Think Your Life is Too Or

Miracle Moments
of Transformation

ELIZABETH KAITES

Front cover photo: Granddaughter Nicole, in Disneyland.
Back cover photo taken by Vivian Storm.

Acknowledgements

Special gratitude goes to Dr. Len Demonceaux and his wonderful partner, Alice, who have hosted our Tuesday group for the past three years. Their love and dedication to personal growth has enabled those of us gathered to choose more positive life behaviors and to grow in spiritual consciousness. His opening challenge, "Any miracles to report this week?" was the impetus for this book. I am grateful that the *Law of Attraction* brought them into my life and they have blessed my husband and me on many levels.

To all of my granddaughters, who continue to inspire me every day with their beautiful spirits and talents. Nicole, my youngest granddaughter, was in rapture at Disneyland, and my photo of her with arms open to all the miracles of life, became the front cover of this book. Vivian is a prospective photography major who took the photograph of the two of us in Colorado that became the back cover of the book. Vivian and her cousin, Eva, who drew the cover of my first book, *A Common Thread: Stories of Our Oneness*, are both photography students and I am so blessed to share this common artistic passion with them.

Genna Herron, my main editor and special friend, is responsible for bringing order out of my writing chaos. She worked masterfully to organize a lot of stories and photographs into a coherent book. It took the love of a friend, in addition to her professional expertise, to pull this off and I am truly grateful. We share a caring heart, healing energy and spiritual consciousness.

My life-long friend, Sue Walker, from Baltimore, spent many Friday mornings on the phone with me reading stories and correcting grammar and sentence construction. I never did get that rule regarding commas right! We were blessed with an excuse to keep in closer touch despite our busy lives. We look forward to spending a few days at the beach to relax and drink a glass of wine or two when the publisher has this book. That will indeed be a miracle moment.

My husband, John, just brought me a 'smoothie' plus an encouraging smile as I type this. His love and support can be seen and read about throughout this book. We know we are blessed in this lifetime and thank our children and grandchildren, as well as friends, for all their love and presence.

If you only knew how many miracles you've already performed, nothing would ever again overwhelm or frighten you.

The Universe

Contents

The sky out my kitchen window.

"Where there is great love, there are always miracles..."
Willa Cather
Death Comes to the Archbishop

To be alive, is to climb the highest mountain, always struggling, not quite satisfied with where you are. Fighting for the right to take one more step, then another, and another. Sometimes we feel as if giving up, easing the struggle, is best. Easier. But still something pulls us on. We are never satisfied until we reach the top, seen all there is to see, and then, only then, do we let ourselves, our fights and pains, go. To be alive, is to struggle, love, hurt, win, lose, fall, rise, run, cry, scream, laugh, breathe, eat, fear, defeat, and... Just Be. To be alive is to be free.
Vivian Storm
Alive

Nothing can dim the light which shines from within.
Maya Angelou

Introduction

I believe humans are living expressions of the Divine and, as such, when we are in alignment, we can allow miracles to flow through us. Now that is something worth realizing! When we choose to let Divine light — or energy — flow through us, as Abraham channels through Esther Hicks, we are in alignment with Spirit, and miracles are common place. Jesus said that what he did we can do, and even more.

For most, a miracle implies that something magical has happened or that something has occurred which we have had no part in, or are at a level of power that our minds cannot comprehend.

I believe neither is true. Miracles are part of our ordinary lives if we just allow ourselves to see them. Our challenge is to be in alignment with the Divine and recognize the truth of who we are and what we can do.

Yesterday a friend returned a copy of the little book I wrote in 2009, *A Common Thread: Stories of our Oneness*. She said, "You need to write more. You tell stories well and, I think, you write about what is important in life."

I thought, "What do I know that is unique or will advance someone else's understanding?"

I have come to know that when I am open and ready to receive, there is guidance to support or inspire me. All of us are challenged in life to be open to those moments that are special and to see the miracles that are always occurring.

I believe one of the truest tests of spiritual maturity is seeing the miraculous in the ordinary. Miracles occur around us all the time, but if you don't know how — or whether — to look for them, you won't see them.

I believe that our world is a reflection of who we are within. As we choose what feelings to have and respond to, we affect the atmosphere around us. Science has determined that we are connected to one another through an energy field. We are more powerful than we realize.

Dr. David Hawkins, and those who have researched the power of prayer groups, speak to how one or a few can affect many. Those from the HeartMath Institute and others speak of the power within our hearts. Our DNA communicates, and our emotions change the shape of our DNA so we can 'co-create' our lives. We cannot choose what happens to us, but we can choose what feelings we will have about those occurrences. Recently there have been studies leading to the belief that we can even change our genes.

The eye-opening miracle is the REALIZATION that we have choices as to our responses to life. Our decision to choose is the real miracle, not the manifestation. Then we can still ourselves and feel the inner guidance always available in us. Interfaith Counseling in Phoenix, Arizona, as well as other helping agencies teach mindfulness as a tool for better coping with life's challenges. Thich Nhat Hanh, a Zen Buddhist teacher, writes in his book, *No Mud, No Lotus*, of stilling the mind as a tool in transformation.

What do miracles have in common? Our asking is an expression of love. The manifestation of a miracle is allowed to unfold as Spirit decides. Then we are to recognize and believe that it has occurred. Within this book are everyday stories of events I have witnessed that seemed to me to illustrate the ordinary miracles and the horizon-broadening experiences to which I am referring. It is my hope that by reading these stories, you will honor similar events in your life.

Together, when we awaken to this Divine mindfulness, we can expand the loving consciousness of our Universe.

I love to take photographs, and the expansiveness of this photo reminds me to broaden my horizons.

Chapter 1:
Beginning the Journey

Tuesday Seekers Group
The Wallet That Returned
Get a Bigger Pan
The Reconnection
Hungry or Full
A Heaven Sent Dog Bite
The Choice

Tuesday Seekers Group

Do you ever have the feeling that you are 'not done?' That there is something yet for you to do in this lifetime? How many of us miss inner guidance, or a strong sense that there is something significant awaiting us?

What influenced me to think about this is my little group of seekers who have been meeting two hours once a week for several years now. The facilitator begins each meeting with the challenge, "Any miracles happen this week?"

I soon came to understand that all of us have something out of the ordinary occurring all the time, but since it isn't a turn-water-into-wine happening, we discount it as special. I believe that when we recognize these happenings, we are empowered to raise the energy in and around us and, thereby, improve our world. One of the truest tests of spiritual maturity is seeing the miracles in the ordinary. Some say this is what it means to be 'awake.' Simply, to me, it means to experience life at its fullest. Miracles occur around us all the time, but if we don't know how — or whether — to look for them they go unnoticed.

In his book, *The Eye of the I*, Dr. David Hawkins suggests that, "For those who have reached higher levels of consciousness, the miraculous is not only commonplace, it is the natural course of events and becomes continuous."

Miracles often occur when they are beyond the reach of negativity and outside the realm of explanation. When we no longer blame others, and stop defending our actions, we live a more positive life. And when we are more likely to be in alignment, miracles result.

Oprah Winfrey, in one of her Super Soul Sunday programs, interviewed the author, Sue Monk Kidd, who wrote *The Secret Life of Bees*. My heart resonated when Sue said, "The spiritual life is so ordinary." They went on to agree that our daily challenge is to *live* our spirituality, and in this alignment with Spirit, create wonderful awareness that we can call miracles.

William Wordsworth stated years ago in *The Prelude*, that there are 'spots of time' when we remember we are divine or that an ordinary occurrence is holy. Our group of seekers constantly challenges each other to know that we are good enough, right here, right now, and that ordinary miracles do occur in our lives. Often one of us recognizes a quality in another that the person was unaware of until that miracle moment. And our attention to it, allows the other to expand in consciousness.

Eckhart Tolle, author of *The Power of Now*, says the only time we have is NOW. The past is gone and the future not here yet, so we can only be alive and affect the world in our NOW. We have the power of choice, of co-creating our lives. Before we realize this, our mind is in control and recreates the familiar. So a miracle coming out of our ordinary lives is the conscious awareness of choice in our NOW, and seeing differently in order to manifest it.

Esther Hicks, an author of *The Law of Attraction*, points out that a miracle occurs when people make a choice for a different way in life, and look at themselves in a new way. Many of us see the manifestation as the miracle; however, the real miracle happens when a person makes the decision to move in a new direction... and has the courage to do so.

It could be that the change is the result of a shift from a *perception* of fear, to a *reality* of love and acceptance. Living a fulfilled life includes recognizing and giving gratitude for these everyday miracles, which leads to a more joyful existence.

```
              Accept -- then act.
       Whatever the present moment contains,
          accept it as if you had chosen it...
       this will miraculously transform your whole life.

                   Eckhart Tolle
              Spiritual author and teacher
```

The story below came to mind one Tuesday when the 'any-miracles-to-report?' question was asked. I replied, "I have one!"

The Wallet That Returned

One Sunday when I stopped at the grocery store on my way home from church, I used a cart to leave the store with a heavy gallon of milk. I returned to my car and off I went. At home, I swung my little Sunday purse up on the closet shelf and went on with my day. Later that afternoon I needed something from my wallet... but it was nowhere to be found. Not in my everyday big purse, not in my Sunday little purse, not in the closet, not on the floor of the car, not anywhere. Panic set in... *my life was in that wallet!*

I phoned the grocery store and was relieved to hear the welcome answer, "We've got it."

I dashed into the store where the beaming woman in customer service said that "one of the kids" had picked up the wallet in the parking lot by the cart racks and turned it in. She didn't know which kid, but my gratitude oozed out to include that wonderful kid, his or her wonderful parents, the wonderful small town we lived in, the wonderful world, etc., etc.

When I returned home, my husband recalled that during the past week, I had received too much change at the local Arby's drive-in window. When I chose to return the correct change to the young man at the window, he thanked me, relieved he would not have to make up the difference at the end of the day. I believe the *Law of Attraction* was at work here with my found wallet. The *Law* says that we attract honesty, kindness, and similar positive emotions when our values are in alignment with those emotions. In simple words, like attracts like, and I had chosen to be honest and return the correct money to the young man. Could there be a connection? I believe so.

There are many letters to the editor in our local newspaper reflecting grateful occurrences like mine. I am writing about MY miracle and the *Law of Attraction* so that YOU can reflect upon your ability to co-create experiences, thus manifesting a more joy-filled life.

People usually consider walking on water
or in thin air a miracle.
But I think the real miracle is not to walk either on water
or in thin air, but to walk on earth.
Every day we are engaged in a miracle which we don't even recognize:
a blue sky, white clouds, green leaves,
the black, curious eyes of a child -- our own two eyes.
All is a miracle.

Thich Nhat Hanh

Get A Bigger Pan

Karen Taylor Good's song, *Get a Bigger Pan*, delighted me at a Sunday morning Unity Church service where she was a guest musician. The song told of a fisherman who kept throwing large fish back into the water when they were too big for his small frying pan. The song suggests that if your habitual actions or thoughts do not allow for growth or challenging opportunities, you need to broaden your horizons and... 'get a bigger pan.'

I was thoughtful after a brief conversation with a former Board member at Unity. I had questioned my value in continuing on the Board as I did not believe my particular skills and interests were needed at that time. My past experiences were those of workshop leadership, starting new programs to deepen spirituality and healing, and communicating more effectively. How could I be helpful in the needed areas of maintenance, finance and organization?

My friend smiled and said, "I felt my time on the Board was an opportunity to serve in ANY way needed."

Those words stayed with me when I was asked to add two items to our church's Wish List at our next Board meeting. Instead of putting those fish in my usual 'small pan' and listing them in the next bulletin and newsletter, I broadened my horizons and got 'a bigger pan' and asked several people to contribute so that we could get the items right away. The church benefited, and I felt useful.

My thanks go out to both Karen — who wrote the words in the song — and the former Board member — who challenged me to grow, step out of the usual and produce a small miracle by responding in a creative way.

Where have you limited your horizons or perceptions of your part to play in life by having too small a pan?

GET A BIGGER PAN!!

A miracle, my friend, is an event which creates faith. Miracles, in the sense of phenomena we cannot explain, surround us on every hand: Life itself is The miracle of miracles.

George Bernard Shaw

The Reconnection

I recall watching a tape recording of Oprah Winfrey's interview with Phil Jackson, the basketball coach who practices Zen and coaches using those principles. He spoke in a calm, peaceful, conscious manner. Could a basketball coach have something to say to us about what is really important in living life successfully?

He stressed the value of team spirit and caring for those with whom we are in community. I thought of Neale Donald Walsh, author of Conversations with God *and who conducts workshops on* Living From Your Soul. *Like Jackson, Walsh stresses that we are part of a community, and it is not enough just knowing your own purpose in life. You are called to challenge others you touch to live the same way.*

We experience events in our lives that we label 'coincidences.' I have come to believe that we attract like-minded people to us, as well as opportunities to be caring and helpful. This story is an example.

I stood up as the train inched its way through the fog into the Newark International Airport station.

"Yes, this is where you get off," acknowledged the woman across the aisle, reading my apprehensive expression. I smiled my thanks as I pulled the strap of my purse over my shoulder, grabbed the handle of my carry-on and stepped down onto the platform.

Following signs into the terminal, I found the American Airlines counter, completed check-in, passed through security, and thankfully settled in the lounge until boarding. My plane was due to leave at 2:45 PM; a glance at my watch showed I had three hours to dig into the latest Jodi Picoult novel.

A few minutes into the story, however, I found my mind wandering back to the past weekend with my son and his wife in New York City. My granddaughter, Eva, had flown in from California, to help set up her mother's art gallery opening. But we also wanted to take in as many sites as we could during our short time together, crisscrossing the city to see Picasso's Marie-Theresa paintings, then resting by the boathouse in Central Park, sipping a Bellini. My son had even treated me to a bike-ped ride in Central Park.

I brushed away a tear as I remembered Sunday, before walking to

a Chinese restaurant for *dim sum*, when we joined other visitors at the Ground Zero Memorial, reading the names of those who lost their lives September 11, 2001.

Then another highlight came to mind and I imagined that Eva will always remember the four of us laughing until our faces hurt at *The Book of Mormon* on Broadway, and the whispers behind us during intermission that caught our attention and we, like every star-struck tourist in the room, stood ogling Robin Williams, Drew Barrymore and Jimmy Fallon also attending this production.

I mused that I had, indeed, been on vacation and smiled at my blessings, grateful that this soon-to-be 76-year-old had managed to keep up with the youngsters!

Such a wonderful time. But now it was over and I was anxious to get back home. My mind returned to the present, and I anxiously peered out the airport window and saw that the fog had not lifted.

DELAYED. Inwardly I groaned when I found my flight on the Departures Board and saw its status.

At 5:30 PM my stomach growled, but my anticipation of a rare first-class seat with dinner, convinced me to put up with the hunger and lose myself again in my book.

Finally, there was the usual activity preceding boarding and I heard, "We're ready to check in our first-class passengers."

More than ready, I was second down the walkway and casually noticed ahead of me a woman dressed in a black suit and crisp white blouse, carrying a large briefcase and walking in long strides. The thought crossed my mind that she must be a high-powered business woman.

As I greeted the attendants at the gangway and entered the plane, I saw Miss Efficiency already in her seat, briefcase under the seat, book in the pocket, seat belt on, and a magazine in her lap. As I stowed my own carry-on and sat in my assigned seat next to her I smiled a 'hello.' No response.

Out of the corner of my eye I could see the diamond rings sparkling on her well-manicured hands as she brushed her hair over her diamond hoop earrings. I turned to introduce myself, but she had buried her head in the magazine, sending a clear signal she was not interested in conversation. I sighed and once again took out my book.

The plane was finally loaded, doors closed, apologies made for the late departure, and we entered the lineup of planes on the runway as number fifteen. The trip from New York to Phoenix loomed long and I wondered if I could nap once my book was finished.

Forty-five minutes later we rose through the clouds into the blue sky above and the attendant came to ask for our drink order.

"I'll have a glass of white wine," I eagerly replied, and my seatmate smiled as she ordered red.

Perhaps the anticipation of sharing a glass of wine allowed her to turn and ask if I lived in Phoenix.

I explained that I had moved north to the small town of Prescott fifteen years ago, and before long we had gotten past the usual polite rituals and she told me she had just sold her practice. When I inquired if she was a physician she replied, "Yes, an OB/GYN who does reconstructive surgery."

"Do you know Isabelle Hagan?" I asked, eager to connect. I had gone to Dr. Hagan, once a year for five years when I lived in Phoenix.

My seatmate turned and looked me straight in the eyes and said, "I am Isabelle Hagan."

As I struggled to close my gaping mouth, she smiled and kindly offered that when you see a person out of their usual environment they look different. Well, it had been fifteen years, but I usually don't forget a face. I remembered that in her office she had dressed with a sort of casual feminine look, and was certainly not adorned with the dazzling diamonds she now wore. Her hair had been loose and flowing and she appeared much younger.

The arrival of the wine helped me compose my thoughts and start anew. Only slightly sputtering, I reminded her that my previous male gynecologist had refused to prescribe hormones until five years after my borderline cancer tumor had been removed, leaving me no alternative to uncomfortable after-affects. She nodded when I said how much I appreciated the wisdom she had given me as she wrote the prescription saying, "There is such a thing as quality of life."

The conversation turned to her as she explained, "I recently retired from practice because arthritis kept me from doing surgery. My husband and I have started a new service, enabling folks to reconnect with spirituality. There are so many people who have left the church of their youth, but haven't reconnected with a spiritual community in their adult lives. We believe this affects their health negatively. We are going to develop a newsletter, and look forward to helping clients."

I told her about the book I had published the year before, and that a third of the book was about the spiritual journey of people and the challenges they encountered along that path. She asked if I would write an article for their newsletter, and I was delighted to say yes.

We did, indeed, have much in common now and as we continued to talk during that long flight the sense of separation dissolved into one of connection and oneness. I told her of starting a healing ministry at my Unity Church in Prescott. I shared with her that there were folks hurting physically and emotionally who were helped by the loving exchange of energy through therapeutic touch in our Sacred Healing Meditation program. We exchanged ideas and goals now that we each were retired. She smiled warmly as we adjusted our trays to receive dinner and another glass of wine.

I was eager to tell her of Barbara Marx Hubbard's *Agents of Consciousness Evolution* training course on the internet developed to catalyze transformation within ourselves, our family and our community. Hubbard believes we need to follow our passions and form small groups of three or more people who can support and encourage each other. We could shift energy toward love and peace in our world instead of fear and divisiveness.

Was it the *Law of Attraction* that allowed us to sit next to each other? Or had we simply chosen to share from our depths to a seeming stranger? Would there be less separation in our world if everyone risked connecting with others who appeared different at first glance?

Lots of thoughts, as well as good feelings about the flight and my seat companion, consumed me as I put my book into my purse. As the plane began its descent, we exchanged cards and agreed that the space around us had been energized with our amazing reconnection.

I was still thinking of Isabelle's new business the following Sunday when we attended church. Was it the *Law of Attraction* that caused a fellow church member to pull me aside and ask if I had time to listen to a situation regarding her daughter?

She spoke of the years of dealing with the daughter's severe depression and how her late husband often prodded the girl to 'suck it up' and get on with life. With tears flowing down her cheeks, she admitted taking their child off the medications prescribed by a local psychiatrist, hoping that positive thinking would transform the sad feelings.

She and her daughter had just returned from California, where at the Amen Clinic, a health clinic that works on treatment of mood and behavior disorders, the daughter had been diagnosed with severe clinical depression. A history of the family confirmed the presence of depression in previous generations and that recovery would be based on treating that inherited condition with medication. They also recommended, based on their research, that family support of this condition and a spiritual component were most effective for successful recovery.

When they suggested her daughter seek a spiritual connection, my friend shook her head and said this last component would be impossible because of a religious experience that had so turned her daughter off from any church.

Feeling hopeful after my reconnection with Dr. Hagan, I wondered if my friend's daughter might be willing to talk with someone in Phoenix who could possibly help with that spiritual component of her recovery.

"She plans to move to Phoenix shortly," my friend said, happily. I was once again grateful for my recent airplane reconnection.

A 'chance' meeting with Dr. Hagan who just 'happened' to be starting a new service to help people reconnect with their spirituality? Listening to a friend at Unity feeling despair for her daughter's recovery because of her negative spiritual experience?

I used to believe in coincidences, but no longer. There is intelligent guidance in our Universe that responds to the *Law of Attraction* and, as a result, sacred occurrences happen and the moment is ready for a miracle.

Remember.... that sometimes not getting what you want is a wonderful stroke of luck.
— Dalai Lama

Hungry or Full?

I heard Oprah interview Dr. Robin Smith, a former therapist and television colleague of hers, who had written a book entitled, *Hungry, The Truth About Being Full.*

Dr. Smith successfully practiced her craft for years, but went through a difficult period in her life when her need to feel better about herself kept her from working. She commented that too often she had 'settled for crumbs' in her life.

Chills went through me when I heard those words. It reminded me that when I was a younger woman, I had successfully practiced my craft as healer and professional helper. But like Dr. Smith, I had often settled for crumbs in my personal life.

I believed others were smarter, more capable, had more exciting lives. Because my perception of my life was distorted by the cultural values of my time — I valued caring for people, beauty, thoughtfulness, sensitivity, service — I allowed others to define my success by their more worldly values. I let my little therapist's life with my company president husband pale in comparison.

Then a few years ago my chiropractor said he wanted a life like mine when he got older. MY LIFE?

He had seen the *reality* of my life... a life full of joy, balance, travel, curiosity, and love.

That lesson taught me to recognize and appreciate the truth of who I was. That I had always been a positive person. That I did not let the challenges in my life keep me down. Nor had I settled for mediocre.

I love myself more now, and that truth is one of my miracles.

Have you discounted the many special occurrences in your life that would have let you know you have a spark of the Divine within? Jesus said, "What I do you can do, and even more." (John 14:12)

What do you believe? Esther Hicks tells us to be in alignment with whom we really are and miracles will happen as a result.

Who are you, really? Could you have a piece of the Divine within and, therefore, be able to be in the alignment that so often allows miracles into your life? Could you be having 'out of the ordinary experiences' often? What is coming to mind?

A Heaven Sent Dog Bite

I began to challenge a long held belief of mine. I thought that I had to work hard to realize good fortune in my life. I love to travel, to see other cultures and learn about different ways of being in this world. To finance my travel, I have led several tours, worked for about two years each on all the details. In addition, whenever I got an opportunity to earn money beyond my regular job, such as a special counseling client or an opportunity to advise unwed mothers at the local high school, I put that money in my 'travel fund.'

I was invited to be a member of a People to People trip to India along with other women professionals. The trip promised a visit with Mother Teresa!

I really wanted to go, but the $4,000 at the time was more than I had.

I volunteered counseling at the local Franciscan Renewal Center, and a friend offered to contribute several thousand dollars to the Center if they would allot $2,000 for my trip. As a result, I was asked to give several talks upon my return.

I could come up with $1,000, so I was just short a final thousand.

Shortly after, on a morning walk, a neighbor's dog came toward me, jumped up and bit me on the thigh. I screamed as I saw the blood running down my leg and — being afraid the dog's larger companion would come out of the yard, too — I managed to hobble home.

My husband rushed me to the emergency room at the local hospital where I got eight stitches.

A week later an insurance representative came to our house, offering me $700 if I would sign papers agreeing not to sue the neighbor who owned the dogs.

"I don't sue neighbors," I replied. And then came inspired guidance: "I'd sign the papers for $1000 though!"

The trip to India was wonderful.

I have come to appreciate, that if I will just expect money to come to support my goals, it will. I don't have to work so hard. Now when it is right for me to do something, the opportunity comes.

A more important question than wondering where the money will come from is, "What is the purpose of the situation, and is it mine to do?"

Mother Teresa challenged each of us to listen to inner guidance when we returned home and choose to respond to our opportunities to do good.

Why did they believe? Because they saw miracles.
Things one man took as chance,
a man of faith took as a sign.
A loved one recovering from disease,
a fortunate business deal,
a chance meeting with a long lost friend.
It wasn't the grand doctrines or the sweeping ideals
that seemed to make believers out of men.
It was the simple magic in the world around them.

Brandon Sanderson
American fantasy and science fiction writer

The whole world is a series of miracles.
But we are so used to them,
we call them ordinary things.

Hans Christian Andersen

The Choice

The second year I worked as chairman in the guidance department at a high school in Maryland, a new man was added to our staff. As I got to know him better, I learned he had studied fine arts in college and got his master's degree in England where he had met and married the love of his life. It was during that magical time that his pregnant wife met a tragic death and, as a result, he lost interest in anything artistic and got a counseling degree.

We became friends and slowly realized we had a shared appreciation of the arts. Eventually, my friend's interests in art led him to notice a young artist named Garry Morrell and offered to sponsor Garry's art exhibits in his home. A few weeks later, he asked if I would like to serve wine and cheese at one of Garry's showings.

I came to love Garry's paintings, but was limited in what I could spend for art (after all, I had four children!). Then one day my friend offered the last original painting that had not sold at the exhibit we had hosted ~ for half price. It felt rather dark and was not very appealing to me. It showed part of a roll top desk, a bird cage with an open door and an open window. I decided to wait until I could afford one of his tree paintings as they reminded me of people, my primary interest in life.

Six months passed and I was invited to my colleague's house for lunch to see Garry's latest painting of a tree. Upon arrival at his Baltimore row house, he ran down the stairs eager to set up dramatic lighting to show off the wonderful 'tree' scene for me.

But when he called, "Come on down!" I didn't. While I had been waiting, something had caught my eye.

I heard him on the steps and turned to him with tears in my eyes when he asked, "What are you doing?"

"I'm buying this painting."

Knowing my obvious lack of interest just a few months before, he looked at me with a puzzled expression on his face, waiting until I could explain.

As we sat down over lunch, we talked about the fact that I had recently filed for divorce. There were so many emotions swirling

around my mind, but when I saw that painting again I made a connection I had not expected could happen six months before.

I had chosen not to stay in the cage of my life. My marriage counselor had a roll top desk. And in my relief at ending my complicated marriage, I had flown out the open window to a new life beyond. The change in me was a miracle and my choice led the children and me into a joyous world.

Don't ask what the world needs.
Ask what makes you come alive and go do it.
Because what the world needs is people who have
COME ALIVE.

Howard Thurman
African American author, philosopher, theologian,
educator, and civil rights leader

Chapter 2:
Early Influences

_____

Early Memories
How About That?
A Decision or a Response to Guidance?
Oberlin and Phil Jackson
Grandmother Was My 'Roll' Model
Family of Artists

Early Memories

My parents were quiet, gentle folks who avoided any strong emotion. My only brother and I were never silly, loud, crazy, or even passionate.

But he and I connected on a different level than our left-brained, scientific parents, and both of us chose psychology majors in college. We also sought out water all our lives as a place where we could go to connect with Spirit, relax and enjoy beauty.

My brother passed away at an early age, so now I go to water to connect my soul with his and with the Divine.

I believe that the entirety of our minds is deep, like the ocean. The ocean is always waving up and down, and is sometimes slow and calm and sometimes stormy.

We're all like the ocean and we think we know who we are, but I suspect our stories aren't big enough. We tend to think we are just a speck in the ocean. What if each of us could transform that image of ourselves as a speck, into one of a powerful wave.

How About That!

I have an early memory of myself at twelve, sitting under an oak tree at church camp in western Pennsylvania. We had just been led in morning devotions by Nettie Dean. Nettie was a heavy-set older woman who radiated joy! She KNEW spirit!

I wanted to glow like Nettie Dean. Nettie had been kind, compassionate, understanding, and caring. She was my spiritual model — the first person in my life to light that fire in my soul.

I never forgot Nettie, and her light still glows in my heart. But it was not until a few years ago when I met with a women's group at a lovely spiritual center in Sedona, Arizona, that I understood the scope of Nettie's influence.

The purpose of these fourteen women was to discuss how they could advance world consciousness. The facilitator began the gathering by asking us to share about our own experiences and about people who had been spiritual role models throughout our lives. She was interested in the people who had inspired us to believe we could make a difference in the world.

When it came to my turn, I talked about how Nettie Dean's love of God had influenced my early life. A woman in the circle gasped and asked if I was from Connellsville, Pennsylvania. She, too, had been brought to a greater sense of love by the same Nettie Dean.

The great revelation perhaps never did come.
Instead there were little daily miracles,
illuminations, matches struck unexpectedly in the dark.

Virginia Woolf
English writer and one of the foremost modernists
of the twentieth century

A Decision or a Response to Guidance?

Most of the women in my family had attended Goucher College in Baltimore. In fact, my socially conscious cousin had been the president of the senior class there when I was a high school senior. Mom told me that Goucher was the number one academically ranked, all-girls school in the United States at that time.

When I asked and was told that Oberlin College was the number one co-ed college, I decided that Oberlin was the place for me.

The dean at our little western Pennsylvania high school told me, "No one from Connellsville High has ever been accepted at Oberlin... and there have been applicants smarter than you!"

Never one to be easily discouraged, I applied. I was so excited to show her my Oberlin acceptance letter.

Was it the *Law of Attraction* that allowed me to be accepted? Did I listen to inner guidance to know what was best for my life?

Or, possibly, was I in alignment with that school's values? As I have said before, I do not believe in luck.

Who am I?

How many of you look back in retrospect and see there is often a clear thread of guidance that was not obvious at the time?

Are these 'out of the ordinary' occurrences easily explained as nothing very unique or amazing to write about?

What if we had understood earlier in our lives that when we listen to inner guidance, we are living the life we came into this world to do, and we receive support from the Universe?

Perhaps when we are passionate about our goals and in alignment, the entire Universe conspires to bring them about.

Oberlin and Phil Jackson

Oberlin had a graduate theology school on campus, and each Wednesday at 10:00 PM, a 20-minute service was held in the small chapel. Seniors took turns sharing thoughts that were important to their lives. I loved that time and the personal sharing of inner wisdom that I heard in those gatherings. Many years later I was a part of creating a similar service on Wednesday evenings in my church community.

How special are those opportunities when we have a peek into the soul of another person. I think when Phil Jackson coached, he opened his heart and soul to his players, and they were raised to another level. Phil spoke of the team spirit, the caring for each other and the determination to enable each member of the team to be his best.

When in your life has there been a person that has seen into your soul and believed in you, or loved you up to another level?

Often in sports an announcer will talk about a player raising his or her game to another level. I am talking about raising your BEING to another level. Oprah Winfrey, in her Super Soul Sunday interviews, points to deepening our Being.

In meditation, a person will experience a depth, a focus, a oneness that is an indicator of 'another level.' Usually these times are unplanned, rather a response to our 'allowing' whatever can happen in the moment. How often do we program stillness into our daily lives and, consequently, receive guidance? What are our choices in books, television shows, friendships, and opportunities for service to others?

Stillness and meditation can be a walk in the woods, prayer, certain music, dreams, or a nap. They are all times when we quiet our minds and can listen.

I am grateful to Oberlin for providing opportunities to be quiet. Many colleges do not value the growth that those quiet times of introspection and soul-searching promote.

And I am also grateful for Phil Jackson, for sharing his unique spiritual coaching style with Oprah.

Elizabeth Kaites, age 75, keeps Grandmother Mattoon's spirit alive as she cooks and bakes with her own eleven grandchildren. You can read more about Elizabeth's grandmother, as well as other fascinating people from her life, by ordering her book of 60 short stories, *A Common Thread, Stories of Our Oneness*, using the Order Form in the back of this book.

Grandmother Was My 'Roll' Model

Grandmother Mattoon lived with us in Connellsville, Pennsylvania, in 1940. The smell of fresh parker house rolls and cinnamon bread baking in the oven brought joy and a feeling of 'all is right with this World-War-Two world.'

"Can I please help Grandmother with the rolls?" I pleaded with my mother. She was more concerned that I spill a speck of flour, a grain of sugar or, worse yet, a precious pat of butter. There was rationing for these necessary ingredients in those days. We had often stood in line at the store for the sporadic shipment of baking items, and Mother did not trust my eager little fingers in the kitchen.

But the kitchen was where my grandmother spent most of her time. Grandfather had died years before and she was reaching the age where her children thought she needed to be closer to them. I know it was hard for her to give up the family farmhouse in Maryland, where folks drove twelve miles from the city, in the days of gasoline rationing, for her Sunday fried chicken and parker house rolls.

My own adventures began while listening to Grandmother on those special occasions when she could talk my mother into letting me in the kitchen. Grandmother had been to New York City to study at Columbia University and had taken a train to get there! She had tales of the wonders of the city and the independent feeling of traveling by yourself.

Years later, she was my biggest advocate when I cleaned out my savings account and went on a 10-week trip to Europe with a college professor and nine other students. That trip changed my life in many ways, and as she rocked in her chair on the front porch, I shared my own tales of traveling on the Paris subway, a train in London and the ship across the Atlantic.

I was a good student and Grandmother understood that I liked people better than math and encouraged me to follow my heart in choosing a major — in psychology. Not the majors, like accounting, that my parents thought would guarantee me a fine living.

Is there any smell yummier than cinnamon and yeast rolls to bring a sigh, and an awareness of love and gratitude in life? A year ago my uncle's daughter wrote and asked if, by chance, I had Grandmother's recipe for parker house rolls. Her dad was ailing and she thought the smell of rolls baking would bring a smile to his pained face and happy memories of his mother. I was happy to send her this recipe.

Grandmother Mattoon's Parker House Rolls

2 cups milk	one yeast cake (2 teaspoons active dry yeast)
3 tablespoons butter	1/4 cup lukewarm water
2 tablespoons sugar	2-1/2 cups flour
1 teaspoon salt	

Scald two cups of milk in a double boiler and pour into a bowl over three tablespoons full of butter, measured level; two tablespoons sugar and one teaspoon salt.

Allow these to stand until lukewarm, then add one yeast cake that has been dissolved in one-fourth cupful of lukewarm water and three cupfuls of flour. Beat hard, cover, and set in a baking pan filled with warm water.

In less than one hour the batter will be a mass of bubbles. Stir down and add two and a half cupfuls of flour. Let stand for half an hour; turn out on a floured board; knead and roll out to the thickness of one-third of an inch.

Cut out with a biscuit cutter dipped in flour. Flour the handle of a knife and make the crease across the center of each roll. Brush each one with butter, fold, press the edges together and lay in a greased pan one inch apart.

Let rise another half-hour and bake in a hot oven (I use 375 degrees) 15 minutes.

Cool on racks and enjoy!

My kitchen is overflowing with cookbooks. I have spent a week with Lorenza de Medici in her Italian kitchen, spent five days with Lydie Marshall at her chateau in France learning French cooking, and been to the Toscana-Mia farmhouse in Italy with my son and daughter for a day in their Italian kitchen.

My children and I love to cook. However, nothing has smelled like heaven, all's right with the world, and love like Grandmother's parker house rolls and cinnamon bread of my childhood. Grandmother has been my role model in many ways. She was independent and chose to live in the country when grandfather got cancer and no longer worked. Grandmother earned money refinishing antiques, doing neighbors' tax returns and sewing doll clothes. And, she always baked food to share with others!

Now, you must excuse me. My heart is yearning for the smell in my own kitchen of those special dinner rolls... and I need to start baking!!

A miracle is a shift in perception from fear to love.
Marianne Williamson

Family of Artists

Looking back, sometimes we can see where our creativity originated. Although my parents were both scientists, my grandfather was an artist. And I am glad to say that my son and several granddaughters are artists. I come from a family of artists.

I, on the other hand, while always appreciating art, wished I could draw but believed any artistic talent had skipped over me. I became a marriage and family therapist, and for years I was both a workshop leader in communication skills and a mentor in a graduate program at a local college.

When I retired, I started traveling and eventually realized that taking photographs was a large part of my traveling enjoyment. Soon I joined a photography interest group in town and taking photographs became my new passion.

A few years into this love affair, a friend came to my home for the first time and politely walked around as one will do, commenting on the lovely energy and beauty in the house. She then stopped short in

front of a small framed photo.

"Oh," she exclaimed, "it looks like a beautiful painted watercolor. I love it!"

Dale Chihuly, the American glass sculptor whose works are considered unique in the field of blown glass and who has a museum in Seattle, Washington, had installed a boat full of colored glass in a pond at the Phoenix Botanical Garden.

For me, the picture was a nice memory of a beautiful day alone with my camera. But as I gazed at the photograph through her appreciative eyes, I could see a boat sitting in a pond surrounded by reeds, smooth water reflecting an amazing display of blown glass. It truly looked like a watercolor painting. It was even similar to one of Grandfather Mattoon's works of art.

My family never really respected my choice of career, but my photography has given me a connection with my grandchildren, and with my friend's comment I claim membership in my artistic family. I made a precious connection that I never had before.

You have a gift that only you can give the world
-- that's the whole reason you're on the planet.
Use your precious energy to build
a magnificent life that really is attainable.
The miracle of your existence
calls for celebration every day.

Oprah Winfrey
American media proprietor, talk show host,
actress, producer, and philanthropist

Chapter 3:
Stories Along the Way

Please Take Her to Lunch
Hot Stuff
An Insightful Sunday
The Johnstown Flood
Hot Fudge Has Bonded Us Forever
Fire-Roasted Tomato Plant
A Big Fish Story
Guidance at the Garage Sale
My Healed Leg Goes to Antelope Canyon
Mary and Me

Please Take Her to Lunch

I was just twenty-two years old, newly graduated from college with a psychology major and it was my first day of work at the Baltimore Welfare Department. I had met with my supervisor, who explained that my job would be to phase out service to 16- to 18-year-old foster care males. I was excited.

However, I was a bit put off when she challenged why I still used 'Betsy' as my name. In her opinion, it was a child's name, or a cow's, or even a name for a car. Since my parents liked the name and I had always been okay with it, I was upset with her challenges.

She was also a bit intimidating. My new — six-foot tall, girlfriend of an Oriole baseball player — supervisor led me to my desk. It was next to a young woman named, Sue, who was asked to please take me to lunch.

Turned out that Sue grew up in a Pennsylvania town only forty miles from where I had lived, and had graduated from Carnegie Mellon the same year as my new engineering husband. Almost sixty years later we are still close friends, having raised our children together and now share stories of our grandchildren.

One of my first counselees was an almost 18-year-old young man. He came into my office with his pipe peeking out of his jacket pocket. He was on his way home from the job he had held at Bethlehem Steel for the past two years. He told me that his dream was to join the Navy the following month when he turned eighteen and receive some training in a skill. His only regret was that he would have to leave his horse.

I was amazed when he came in for his appointment the week after his birthday. Instead of a happy face, he had a sad one. The Navy had turned him down because he had 'a record.' He had robbed a gas station for eighty-seven cents when he was fourteen, and was running away from an abusive foster family. This was his only record. The recruiter had told him he would need someone to speak for him in order for them to reconsider.

Did I mention that the Baltimore Welfare Department had a policy that counselors like me could not leave the building during work hours? Well, I phoned the Navy recruiter and asked if I could go in and 'speak for Tom,' would that help his case? I rushed over the next day on my 30-minute lunch time, put up with the laughs of the Navy recruiters who said, of course, they would take this young man who had all kinds of evidence of responsibility, even if told by a young girl like me. They further said that most applicants had a parent or a minister speak for them, but Tom said he had no one.

They had never had a welfare counselor come in to plead the case of a person before. And I had never been called in to be reprimanded by a department head before. But I was when I returned to work that day. Even so, I was surprised when my supervisor was fired, and I was now to report to her supervisor. He said not to feel too bad, that my incident had been the 'last straw with that woman.' She had been reprimanded before because of her priorities, that her 'policies' were more important than the needs of the clients.

Months later, my new supervisor was supportive when Sue and I approached him with our plan to offer counseling to unwed women who were currently receiving welfare aid for each new pregnancy. He was open to ideas that expanded helpful services.

I was joyful when I received letters from my 'oh so happy' Navy friend about all his training — and later, his successes.

I don't know whether this was an indication of my willfulness, or an innate feeling that if a rule kept you from doing what your heart and soul felt was right, then you were justified in taking action, even if you risked a consequence. That young man gave me an opportunity to expand my heart and I am still grateful for his presence in my life.

Once you believe in yourself
and see your soul as divine and precious,
you'll automatically be converted
to a being who can create miracles.

Wayne Dyer
American philosopher, self-help author
and a motivational speaker

Hot Stuff!!

It was the Super Bowl, World Series and All-Star Game all wrapped into one the night the Connellsville Joint Senior High girls played their Yale/Princeton game. I was a sophomore forward and since only the best players were chosen for the once-a-year basketball game, I thought I was hot stuff!

The whistle blew the start of the game, the teens in the overflowing stands roared their support and I could hardly contain my excitement. My team uniform was orange and black, like the real Princeton College players. The first quarter ended and my main contribution was passing the ball to Connie Conway, our best player. The score was close and as the second half neared its end, Connie passed the ball to me and I scored... not once but twice!!

I glanced up to the stands where I had seen my boyfriend before the game started. I was sure he had a proud smile on his handsome face and was looking forward, as I was, to the dance at the conclusion of the game. After the game, I went into the locker room with the rest of the team, pleased that I had scored three points.

Funny, but I don't remember if our team won or not. It was the one night that the girls got to play a game in the gym at night. That made it special enough, and I had made the team!

I married that high school boyfriend and we shared nineteen years and were blessed with four children. However, as often happens in life, we grew apart, had challenges as to who we were inside, and divorced. Later, I remarried.

I believe that we have choices as to how we deal with both the opportunities and the challenges in our lives. The more we connect to our inner Divinity — our real Hot Stuff — the greater our alignment and joy-filled life.

Be realistic: Plan for a miracle.
Osho
Indian mystic, guru and spiritual teacher

An Insightful Sunday

As Dr. Jill Bolte Taylor was recounting her 'stroke of insight' experience on television one Sunday, I flashed back to a morning in Baltimore, years before, and felt a shiver go up my insides. She was recalling being unable to articulate because of hemorrhaging in her left brain while being aware of language and thought in her right brain. In other words, she was having a stroke.

I was transported to a morning when I held my baby son in my left arm while wielding a vacuum cleaner with my right. The bright sunlight on that snowy day nearly blinded my vision of our driveway outside. When I answered the ringing telephone, I struggled to say, "Hello." I was aware of the word somewhere in my head, but gibberish came out of my mouth.

A searing pain swept across my head as I stood in the kitchen, uncertain as to what was happening, and scared about what to do. I put Steve in the playpen beside his one-year-old sister and tried to remember my husband's work number... then ANY number! My neighbor's number finally came to me, and when she answered I mumbled, "Help."

She came running and put me to bed while she tended to the three-year-old who was playing cars in his room, the five-year-old in her room with her books, and the babies in the playpen.

My husband came home from work, a call was made to my doctor, and I was on my way to the hospital. After a solid week of testing, including a spinal tap that put me flat on my back for days, the doctors came to the conclusion that I had experienced a reaction to the birth control pills. Birth control pills were new back then, and came with side effects not completely known, but a Godsend to me since I had become pregnant with my fourth child having used the only two methods of birth control available at that time.

My chart was stamped with NO BIRTH CONTROL PILLS, and I was released to go home.

It was a stressful time in my life, since my brother had recently become engaged to the only child of a Massachusetts physician who happened to be Robert Kennedy's doctor. My parents were awed by this prospective union, and I was to hold the bridal shower since I lived halfway between their home and Massachusetts. Why, my mother had telephoned just to make sure my wedding china had no chips and we hadn't broken any of the crystal goblets she planned to use.

And my 'medical incident' was all but forgotten. Mother and Dad could not understand how anyone in our family could have had FOUR children. Needless to say, they were embarrassed. Mother had even told me that if I got pregnant again, to find someone else to come and help while I was in the hospital.

The children were a joy in my life, and we had a spacious house in the country, down the lane away from the road. My husband and I had designed and built the house ourselves, and I was proud that we had — with Joe doing a lot of the work himself and tightly managing the bills — completed the building with only a $600 overrun. I could show you photographs of the picnics we had when I brought dinner out to the house where my husband was taping and spackling drywall, the children were pedaling tricycles on the concrete flooring, and I was taking seeds out of the watermelon before the crawling toddler put the slices in his mouth.

But as much as I loved that house, I was stressed planning the shower for my brother because so much was unfinished! I had saved enough money so we could have another load of stones put on the long lane from the road to the house before the special bridal shower. A muddy entrance would be unacceptable. Mother was to arrive the day before from Ohio to help set the table and put out the fancy goodies. My neighbor had offered to take the three youngest children for the afternoon.

Believe it or not, all went well! The sunshine was outside and in, and the family proceeded to plan for the wedding.

Years later, I received a master's degree, held a good job, survived a divorce, and remarried. My second husband moved us into a lovely home in another state. My new stepchildren were a special joy.

But shadows of that long ago morning in Baltimore continued to haunt my life, even without my recognizing them. My new engineer husband would get frustrated and tease me about my inability to handle tools or much of anything that required left-brain motor ability. He often would shake his head in amazement that anyone as smart as I could not remember how to use a jar opener, deal with putting new caps on outside emitters, etc., etc! I recounted that I just didn't have much of a left brain. This book is even full of stories that my editor says I had all over my computer, not in the files (or were they folders?) where she had asked me to place them.

In my professional work as a therapist, I was able to listen to clients and also understand their patterns of thought and intervene helpfully. Once, a well-known psychologist I worked with who had evaluated many counselors, said I was especially able to be intuitive (right-brain skills), and gave me great opportunities to travel with him and do weekend workshops. So I felt adequate.

That Sunday, while listening to Dr. Jill, I realized that she was describing some of what I had experienced those many years before. Could my left-brain deficiencies be traced back to what is now referred to as a Transient Ischemic Attack (TIA)? That would explain my symptoms and seeming recovery because with a TIA the blood flow to part of the brain is blocked or reduced, often by a blood clot. After a short time, blood flows again and the symptoms go away. Could I have over-developed my right brain and, as such, been a loving light of help to many clients, friends and family? Thank you, God!

I am safe and secure.
I exhale any anxiety and inhale calm.
As my world expands, so do my heart and mind.
I am willing to stay open and accept
all the miracles and abundance
the universe has to offer me.
Kris Carr

The Johnstown Flood

You've probably heard about the great Johnstown Flood of 1889, which swept away over 2,200 people when the dam broke after heavy rains. Well, I was close to being swept away in the great Johnstown flood of 1977!

Johnstown is a southwestern Pennsylvania city built along the banks of the Conemaugh River, where John worked and had an apartment. We had recently been married and put a down payment on a house.

Because of its typographical location beside the Conemaugh and nestled in the Laurel Mountains on both sides, it was often cloudy and rainy in Johnstown all year. I later read that Johnstown gets an amount of yearly precipitation second only to Seattle.

So we had decided to rent a house about 25 miles south of Johnstown at Indian Lake for the summer. With a wooden boat to paddle around in and a motor boat to try to rev up enough to pull water skis, all of our kids were happier at the lake... and renting that house probably saved our lives.

It was the usual dark and gloomy day when we left our lake house on that fateful morning. We were driving to Baltimore to see my counseling clients and to take my two sons to visit their father at the Jemicy School, where he taught.

Clients seen and a father visited, the three of us departed Baltimore about 10:00 PM for the three-hour drive back home. As we left Maryland and approached the Pennsylvania Turnpike, the drizzle turned to hard rain. Soon we were shuddering at the constant lightening bolts and roars of thunder. The rain beat against our little Volkswagen bug, the windshield wipers struggled valiantly to keep up but I could hardly see to forge ahead. The boys were alert, not their usual sleepy selves on this late night drive.

"Should we stop until it lessens?" I thought to myself, but I slowly drove on, just wanting to get safely home and not stranded on the side of the road.

I turned on the car radio to drown out the thunder claps, but to no avail. The static was painful. I had never been in a storm where the lightening was continuous.

We made it to our exit, but instead of turning toward Johnstown, we started up the mountain toward Indian Lake. The rain kept up, but the lightening lessened as we approached our lake house.

By the time we got home, it was almost 1:30 AM. I kissed the boys goodnight, grateful that it was summer and no school the next day. The only thing I had to do the next day was take John's son for a lesson in Johnstown at 10:00 AM.

My husband had driven down after work that day, and as I slipped into bed, he stirred. "I guess you're grateful that we made it home in this horrible weather!" I said.

Just, "Em," came from him as he turned over and continued sleeping.

The boys were still asleep when I glanced at the clock on my way to the bathroom... 9:15 AM. John was long gone on his way to work. Then the phone started ringing insistently.

"Don't leave or go anywhere!" my husband's excited voice shouted. "Johnstown's FLOODED! I'm on my way back to the lake as the roads into town are all blocked. I looked down over the Westmont hill and saw our office building under water."

He and two colleagues were erecting a new building and the construction was about halfway up the first floor. My, I was glad it wasn't further along.

When he arrived at the lake house, the boys and I were up and eager to hear the news. About 1:30 AM last night, the main road into town was blocked as a car had gone into the rising river.

Wow. I realized that if I had driven into Johnstown the night before, I would have been on that main road at that exact time.

Thank you, God!

Don't believe in miracles -- depend on them.

Laurence J. Peter
Canadian educator and 'hierarchiologist'
best known to the general public for the
formulation of the Peter Principle

Hot Fudge Has Bonded Us Forever!

How do you really get to know a daughter's fiancée? We had heard about this young man who had met our daughter in Boston when he arrived at Tufts University and had applied to be a dorm proctor. Daughter Joedy was in charge of this program, which hired older students to live in the dorms with the newbies. Mike had come from Honolulu to work on an advanced degree at Harvard. Not one to waste his money on fancy digs, he chose to come over to live and work at the underclass dorm at neighboring Tufts.

We had been told that Mike had climbed the tallest peaks in every continent, that he was a fourth generation Chinese who taught chemistry at the Punahou School in Honolulu, and that he 'was cute.'

When the courtship resulted in an engagement ring, we looked forward to their spending spring break with us. I planned a bridal shower for one afternoon to introduce our daughter to my friends, and looked forward to meeting this man who would become family.

At the time, we lived in an Arizona house that was quite large and had a swimming pool. Mike later told me that he had wondered how I would feel about his more simple family. He brought me a box of chocolates and said that he loved chocolate and hoped I did too. I sure did!

May came quickly and we left several days before the wedding being held at the Tufts Chapel. Joedy was still working, so when I asked Mike what I could do to help, he said I could be the most help by helping him clean the second floor rooms of the dorm where they were housing the soon to be arriving friends and family members coming to the wedding. Unfortunately, the University had discovered asbestos in the dorm ceilings and were planning to remove it in all the dorms. They therefore were not going to clean up rooms immediately after the students left for the summer.

If any of you have teenage boys, you can imagine the state of those rooms. Dust from September, single socks thrown on the floor, old tennis shoes which had been replaced months before, magazine pages ripped out and stomped on many times and, of course, coins, mostly pennies that were not worth bending over and picking up!

Mike brought me a broom and dust rag and I started down one side of the hall while he took the other. He came to check and see if I was up to the task and was surprised at my progress. Then I got the best idea! Perhaps we'd each pocket enough change to treat ourselves to a hot fudge sundae when we finished our work!

The next time he came over to check on me, I told him my plan and he was excited! He, too, had pocketed the coins he had found on the floor.

We soon accumulated a pile of the nice things left — like radios and good sweaters out in the hall and decided to give them to the custodian to pass along wherever. But we didn't pass on our coins.

At the end of the hall, we agreed that the rooms were fit for the families and friends, and we eagerly counted our change. I had $2.68 and Mike had $3.29. Surely enough for ice cream!

At the shop, we both ordered hot fudge, agreeing that there was nothing better.

Mike says that my willingness to clean those filthy rooms caused him to decide I was OK as a future mother-in-law. I believe it was the game we played with the coins and our mutual love of hot fudge.

He is a great son-in-law. Always

up for fun, a dinner out at a nice restaurant that, of course, has delicious chocolate desserts, is a loving husband to Joedy, and a fine father to our grandchildren. He went from Punahou to a private Baptist high school where he has raised the standards of that little school. I feel a loving bond across the ocean to Honolulu from our Arizona home.

To me every hour of the light and dark is a miracle,
every cubic inch of space is an unspeakably perfect miracle.
Seeing, hearing, feeling, are miracles,
and each part and tag of me is a miracle.

Walt Whitman

The Fire-Roasted Tomato Plant

Growing plants in pots on our deck is my idea of older-age gardening, but not my husband's. John keeps saying, "We could buy fruits and vegetables at any grocery store or farmer's market and save both time and money."

"But they don't TASTE the same," is my heated plea.

My engineer husband, an efficiency expert in his working days, carefully evaluates the costs, whereas there are times when I will pay for better quality and the joy of seeing my plants grow.

Our next door neighbor agrees with me about the taste, as well as the challenge of being a city farmer, but always warns, "Don't plant anything outside here in Prescott, until after Mother's Day."

Despite the fact that we live in sunny Arizona, it has been known to snow in early May.

Recently, my inventive husband figured out how to rig up a drip system connected to an outside faucet, so he could water my pots every other day and not have to carry pails of water out to the deck. If this garden is my idea, you might ask, why don't I water the little darlings?

Well, John seems to take delight in regulating the outside watering needs in order not to risk wasting money I might spend on the 'garden.' In my opinion, our tomatoes and peppers last year were a real joy to eat and just about the right amount for us.

That year the owner of our local garden center came to the women's association meeting at our church. Watters Garden Center had just won an award for having Arizona's best garden center. The owner was excited to be at our meeting and encouraged us to read his weekly column in the local newspaper.

In April, his column about tomatoes caught my eye: "Our shipment of Big Boy tomato plants has arrived and are ready to plant."

I was excited.

He went on to say that one plant would produce many pounds of tomatoes from June through the summer as the plants were sturdy with a few buds already on their beautiful green leaves.

I was sold.

When I went to the center, there were dozens of healthy-looking Big Boy tomato plants and I cautiously asked if it was too early to put a plant out on our deck because it wasn't Mother's Day yet.

"You should be all right now," was the eager salesman's reply.

With a look of 'why don't we just buy tomatoes this year instead of babying this plant,' John got out the mulch, put on his garden gloves and asked me to bring the hand spade out to the big clay pot we used for our annual tomato plant. It was a lovely spring day and I imagined that we were having a fine time. After all, John only had one plant to deal with.

I was eager to tell our grandson about our plants. Ten-year-old Jacob lived in Phoenix, and was the farmer in our family. He bragged about his blueberries when we talked, and I knew he had already planted his tomato plant. I was looking forward to showing him my garden on his next visit.

During the next week, John and I looked out on the deck at our Big Boy, hearty and healthy, as its leaves waved to us in the breeze. The drip system was doing its work and Big Boy was happy in the company of the blueberry, raspberry and spinach plants already in pots on our deck garden. I smiled wider as I sat in my home office and gazed out the window at my garden. I love to cook and had picked leaves from my spinach plant that morning for lunch. I was eager for the day when I could pick a fresh tomato to add to the salad.

It was two weeks before Mother's Day when I became concerned about the gray sky and colder temperature. No, no, please, no snow! John came in to say that he had just heard that snow was forecast with freezing temperatures and I asked him, "What shall we do?"

"Well, we'll just have to bring the tomato plant into the house," John advised, sighing. Carefully, we opened the door to the study and half lifted and half pushed the big pot into the room.

Craaaaaack, the big pot complained as we dragged it from the deck, up the step and over the threshold of the door. Expecting a trail of dirt on the carpet, we were relieved to find upon investigation that the noise was only coming from the tray under the pot.

The big pot was totally blocking the door to the deck. Our dog kept watching us, head tilted to one side with an anxious expression on her face – less concerned, I'm sure, at our huffing and puffing as we struggled with that clay pot than about the interruption of her routine of being let out the kitchen door instead of the deck door to do her business.

The snow came and went and we shoved and heaved the pot back out onto the deck, thankful we saved the life of Big Boy. Once again I could smile while typing a story on my computer and gaze out the window at my deck garden. The spinach plant was replenishing itself and we had a cheese and spinach omelet for breakfast one morning. How wonderful it will be when we can add a fresh tomato from our garden.

A week later, now just days before Mother's Day, I was distressed to hear that the next day there was a chance of snow again. Glory, I was afraid that another move might really crack the big pot, or at the least, John's patience. What were we to do?

I went into the hamper where we keep old towels, ripped clothes and holey blankets. I got out a lightweight towel for good measure and an old play pen cover that caused a light bulb go off in John's mind.

He called our neighbor, Earl, to see what he thought of putting a real light bulb in the pot, under the play pen cover, to keep Big Boy warm that night since the temperature was to go below freezing.

"Sounds okay to me," said Earl. "Just make sure you make a tent so the bulb doesn't touch anything."

Looking out the window that afternoon we saw the snow squalls beginning. So early. John turned on the rescue light bulb. I was impressed that John cared enough to protect the plant and had come up with an idea that intrigued him. Whatever would interest him made me happy. I had an afternoon class at church to attend and he had a quick trip to the hardware store in mind, so off we went.

At five o'clock when I returned from class and walked in the house I immediately noticed the acrid smell of smoke ~ it was overpowering! Running into the study, I asked John, who was calmly sitting on the couch, what happened.

"I nearly burned the house down," he said with a chagrined smile. "What??"

Quickly he explained he had come back from the store, followed the smell and discovered flames rising from the blanket over the tomato plant and shooting up the side of the house. Even the dead grass under the wooden deck was on fire!

"Oh, my God!" I exclaimed and opened the deck door in amazement and horror. I could see the hose lying on charred deck flooring following John's efforts at hosing down everything trying to save the house.

Exhausted, with a smudge of soot still on his face, John slowly made it to the door, looked over at me and shook his head, "All this to save a $25 tomato plant."

After awhile we were able to talk quietly about what happened, breathing sighs of relief and expressing our gratitude. If not for the afternoon snow flurry, we would have gone to bed with the light under the blanket. We shuttered to think what would have happened while we slept.

But I imagine this will be a good story for years to come on how much it cost to repair the house after trying to save my Big Boy from freezing. I doubt there will be another tomato plant allowed at this house ~ after Mother's Day or ever again.

Now I look out the window and see the leaves of the blackberry and blueberry plants waving at me. And I can see smoke damaged siding on the house, a black pot.... and a completely *fire-roasted tomato plant!*

I've written about having choices. Sometimes we make mistakes. Do we learn from them and not defend them? Whenever possible, how about righting the wrongs, making changes and transforming our situations into ones of love and gratitude. I have found that this is even better than being right.

When the fire of your soul
ignites the passion with your heart,
don't view it as a chance for success or failure,
view it as an open door for miracles.
Jennifer Finney Boylan
American author, political activist and Anna Quindlen Writer-
in-Residence of Barnard College of Columbia University

A Big Fish Story

Where could he be? It was his birthday, and he was late coming to our unit at Pacifica Club. It was Thanksgiving Day and we had made a reservation at the only restaurant in Ixtapa, Mexico, that served a traditional American turkey dinner. Mary, our daughter, said that her husband told her that he'd be home early, about 2:00 PM.

Our reservation was for 7:30 PM and it was almost 5:00. Our concern was heightened by the fact that he was recovering from a knee replacement and was using a cane... just the clue that unsavory characters would need to 'jump' someone, out alone by the docks. He had gone fishing, leaving before dawn, with his usual guide on a small, one-customer boat. Keith, an outdoor guy – so able to take care of himself – couldn't imagine anybody worrying.

Marika, one of our 16-year-old twin granddaughters climbed up on the top bunk and looked out the window, which gave her a good view of the street where she could see a taxi.

"Dad knows we have a birthday reservation at the restaurant," she said worriedly.

Mary and her dad decided to go down to the office and call over to the dock for any information. When they were told that all the boats were in, Mary shed a tear, "Why hasn't he called?"

Mary was sure that the boat captain had a cell phone. By now it was close to 7:00 and growing dark.

I took the other twin over to the restaurant, where we told them of our dilemma. They suggested that we make a reservation for the next night, since there were others eager to eat a turkey dinner and take our place. We said to hold on until 7:30 PM and then seat others.

"Grandmom, I'm starving," Megan said, so we rode the tram down to the beach restaurant. I pleaded our case for carry-out to the waitress as her eyes reflected her concern and compassion. We rode up the tram with two big boxes of dinner apiece. No turkey, however, and definitely no birthday cake.

By now we were all frantic and no one else but Megan could eat a bite. I heard sobs coming from the top bunk as dark came and no taxi stopped in front of our unit. We had been coming to Ixtapa for eight years on Thanksgiving and had always had a wonderful time.

This was different. We knew Keith to be a strong and resourceful man, but he was not his usual robust self with his knee and cane. Surely he would have called if he could.

My husband and Mary climbed up and down the six or so flights of stairs to the office and called the police. No word of an accident, but they'd call if anything turned up.

Our minds kept coming up with worst-case scenarios. Keith was over six feet tall, much bigger than the small Mexican boat captain who would not have been able to pull Keith into the boat if he had lost his balance and fallen overboard. In the darkness of Zihuatanejo, where the boat was kept, on a Thursday night, would anyone help if someone robbed him?

All those thoughts ran through our minds as we waited and chewed our nails. It was hard to stay positive.

"Was that a car door?" shouted Marika, as she raced to the door.

Shouts of "Daddy, Daddy!!" reached our ears as a smiling Keith entered the room. Eagerly starting to tell us of his adventure, he first had to calm a crying wife, relieved twins, a puzzled mother-in-law, and a growing-angry father-in-law.

His face was flushed with excitement as he began. "I hooked a huge marlin about 11:00 AM and it took seven hours to pull him into the boat. Man, I'm exhausted!"

Apparently, all the boats had not come in when we called. Theirs had still been out.

"Wow, the folks at the dock took pictures and folks said it was one of the biggest catches of the season!" exclaimed an excited and glowing Keith.

My husband questioned why he hadn't called to explain his delay. "We were too busy holding onto the line!"

"And when you got to the dock?" Mary challenged.

"It never entered my mind that you would worry," exclaimed macho Keith.

Now hungry and eager for his birthday dinner, Keith yelled, "Let's go now!"

No one else was hungry or ready to go. It was after 9:00 PM by then and bed seemed more inviting than food to my husband and me. The twins were tired from worry and Megan was full from the beach food.

Mary and Keith settled for a walk and then bed. By the time they returned, Keith had finally 'gotten' it and promised that if there was a future delay he would remember to call. Dinner the next and last night of our trip seemed anti-climatic somehow.

Most fish stories are about the one that got away. This was different. Our miracle was a safe Keith who had a great fish adventure on his birthday.

Years later, John and I now know that the best thing we can do in a similar challenging situation, is to send love and protection. Worrying or any negative emotion will not help. The *Law of Attraction* lets us know that our positive feelings will attract good results. We were blessed that Keith's joy was stronger than our concern.

> The key to seeing the world's soul,
> and in the process wakening one's own,
> is to get over the confusion by which we think
> that fact is real and imagination an illusion.
> It is the other way around.
> Fact is an illusion, because every fact
> is part of a story and is riddled with imagination.
> Imagination is real because every perception
> of the world around us
> is absolutely colored by the narrative
> or image-filled lens through which we perceive.
> We are all poets and artists
> as we live our daily lives,
> whether or not we recognize this role
> or whether or not we believe it.
>
> Thomas Moore
> American psychotherapist, former monk, writer of
> popular spiritual books, and lecturer in the fields of
> archetypal psychology, mythology, and imagination

I believe in pink
I believe that laughing
     is the best calorie burner

I believe in being strong when everything
     seems to be going wrong
I believe that happy girls
     are the prettiest girls
I believe that tomorrow is another day
     and I believe in miracles.

Audrey Hepburn

Guidance at the Garage Sale

I had been looking in the garage sale section of the newspaper for outdoor patio furniture. Our daughter's pool and backyard renovation for their new Arizona retirement house was almost done, and since it was the end of summer, I was hoping to find some pieces for sale at a reasonable price.

My eye was drawn to a simple ad for a five-piece wicker set. I told my daughter-in-law, who lives in Phoenix about my 'find' and asked her advice. She commented that wicker wouldn't hold up in the Phoenix heat. But somehow, I kept thinking about the newspaper ad.

My husband and I were going near the address on our way to a movie, and he agreed to stop and indulge me in what he thought was a useless side trip. It was a lovely sunny day and the attractive, thin and peppy woman who came out of the garage intrigued him enough to get out of our car. She led me to the set which was in perfect condition, just a bit old fashioned in its seat cushion fabric.

I sighed as I commented that our daughter was looking for a more sleek set and, besides, it probably wouldn't hold up in the Phoenix heat.

But instead of being relieved the matter was settled and we could go on our way, to my surprise John moved closer to the woman and asked her age.

To her reply he commented, "You are certainly a young looking 80-year-old."

I muttered that she was only six months older than me.

"But, fifteen pounds lighter," came his response.

Now I was the one who moved closer to our car, more than ready to leave.

"Well, thanks for letting us look," I said.

We stopped for a quick McDonald's, and he raved at the quality of the furniture, the neatness of the tools on the garage wall and the sprightliness of the woman. One would think that I had had enough of this furniture quest but, in fact, I liked the set and it stayed in my mind.

I awoke the next morning thinking of friends who had just moved into a house in the country. They had a little front porch which they planned to enlarge so they could view the vast expanse of Flagstaff's three peaks off in the distance.

My usually frugal husband looked at me and said, "Why don't we buy that set for them?"

What a perfect outcome! But, I went alone to pay her.

We had had fun finding the furniture, enjoyed meeting the owner and being guided to give it to our friends. My gift that day was to be grateful for my inspiration to find a home for the furniture and not brood over my husband's comment about my weight! I love knowing that I co-create my reality by my choice of emotions and perception.

Don't fall for a magic wand,
we humans got it all... we perform the miracles.
Kate Bush
English singer-songwriter, musician and record producer

My Healed Leg Goes to Antelope Canyon

She was a member of our church and then we were fellow writers. My husband and I traveled to the city of Kingman, Arizona, when she was in ministerial school and where she started a church. We would give a talk and then enjoy hearing of her work over lunch.

Graduation came and this former occupational therapist returned to our town to live and work, just in time to stay with us when I needed help in recovering from a broken leg. So as you can see, our hearts were connected.

This year, one of my birthday wishes was to go to Antelope Canyon and take photos. She agreed to go with me, and hold out a helping hand if I needed it!

Up north we journeyed, and my Tuesday group 'blew away any clouds' so I could get a photograph of the ray of light possible on the canyon floor at noon. As you can see, all was in place for my wish to come true.

I hope you can feel the glow still present in me from this opportunity of soul connection.

Light is symbolic to me. You and I are the light in the world. My photograph of the beam in the Canyon is a treasured memento of how, letting light shine, helps to transform the world.

Mary and Me

Her dad will be ninety years old this summer. She and I have been plotting and exploring and planning the celebration. He doesn't much care what is done.

"Just don't do much," he says.

Many things are hard for John and me these days. We don't eat as much, we don't stay up as late, we rarely go out in the evening; we don't entertain as much, we don't travel as much — we're older now!

So the cake can't be too sweet, paper plates will be easier to deal with, can't have grandkids sleep on mattresses on the floor anymore, and what will we do if it rains? After all, it's July and we live in Arizona where the monsoons arrive most days.

It's hard to believe that her dad and I have been married for forty years now. I still remember hearing about her wedding the summer after her college graduation. A colleague of mine couldn't stop talking about the Greek wedding she had attended and how fun to see the grandparents do the traditional handkerchief dance.

Months later I was introduced to her dad after my colleague had a dream where we were together. I didn't meet his daughter, Mary, until the grandfather who danced at her wedding passed away and I drove from my home in Maryland to the funeral in West Virginia.

We've had many wonderful times vacationing together — house boating on Lake Powell, Thanksgiving in Ixtapa, Mexico, trips to her house in Colorado and to ours in Arizona... and a mud bath in New Mexico.

And we have many memories of birthdays and Christmases together.

But, as I said, it's forty years later and both her dad and I are older. She and her husband have aged as well and several years ago bought a second home for their future retirement in Arizona, just over an hour's drive from us. And when they tired of the snow and ice at their home in Colorado, they came down to sunny Arizona to plan their future, full-time life here.

Mary started driving up to Prescott to spend one day a week with us. Lunches out soon transitioned into, "How can I help you this week?"

Plants outside got trimmed, closets got better organized, and trips to Goodwill ensued.

Now the focus is on this 90th birthday celebration.

What the blessing is in all this is how much fun she and I are still having! We are on the same page with decisions, and enjoy creating invitations and making necessary reservations.

I don't know about other families, I just know that my stepdaughter and I are having MUCH fun doing what families do!

We must not allow the clock and the calendar to blind us to the fact that each moment of life is a miracle and mystery.

H.G. Wells

Chapter 4:
My Family

————————————————————————————————

Lesson From a Five Year Old

My older son, Paul, has had difficulty valuing his more sensitive personality characteristics in his life, but this story shows he has always been in alignment with a spiritual consciousness.

He was in kindergarten. One day an invitation came in the mail for him to attend a classmate's birthday party. I commented that I had never heard him mention this boy before.

"Oh, he doesn't have any friends. He is really fat and can't play with the rest of us at recess. The other kids laugh at him. I don't really know him, but I want to go to his party as I'm not sure anyone else will."

As feared, he was the only other attendee.

"His mother made the best cake, and look at the bag of treats she gave me to bring home.

"We had a good time playing a board game and I know him better now. I'll be sure to talk to him at school from now on."

I had never been more proud of my son.

You want to see a miracle? Be a miracle.

Morgan Freeman
American actor and narrator

Transformation of a Disaster

When Paul was in kindergarten, Braddock, Pennsylvania, was the most prosperous town in the Pittsburgh area. You might say, it was the Silicon Valley of the steel industry.

However, this story is about both Paul and Braddock fifty years later. Paul is an art professor at Pennsylvania State University, happily married and the father of Eva, a graduate photography student at Yale.

Braddock has lost ninety percent of its population and its shoe-string steel mill is the last remaining one in operation in the Pittsburgh region. Ted Talks has a video of John Federman, the tattooed, six-foot, eight-inch Harvard PhD graduate, who ran for mayor of Braddock... and won by one vote. He campaigned saying that Pennsylvania had an opportunity with Braddock to show the rest of the country how a city could start over with new goals and regain its life after industry changed its needs. We hear of the challenges of the auto industry in Detroit, the coal industry in West Virginia and others.

Braddock's story continues... when a Carnegie Mellon graduate came to Braddock and bought a building. He worked with the mayor to attract artists to display their work. Paul was approached to present a show with an African American colleague. This was to be an urban renewal project to show that Braddock was a laboratory for idealistic transformation. Young people were offered houses at low prices, craftsmen taught kids to make things out of the volume of scrap metal in the town and various ethnic groups were working together.

Why this story in my book? Well, it occurs to me that this son, Paul, who was sensitive to a fellow kindergartener many years before, is still sensitive to being a positive agent for transformation. As each of us responds to the challenges in our lives, we can help transform disasters into triumphs.

A Son's Story

The phone rang and I heard news that any parent dreads. My son, nine-month-pregnant daughter-in-law and two-year-old grandson had been in a head-on collision as they were returning from a Sunday afternoon baby shower.

The driver was drunk and forced them off a steep embankment. Steve had managed to angle the car so his driver's side had taken the brunt of the impact. But the helicopter EMTs feared he would not survive until they reached the hospital.

Our first miracle... my grandson, Trevor, was removed from his child seat unscathed and was bundled off with friends who had been at the baby shower and stopped their car to help.

As a result of the crash, her water had broken sending my daughter-in-law immediately into labor. Our second miracle? She had given birth to a healthy girl during the night and was traumatized but, thank God, both were going to be all right.

Steve, however, was in critical condition with every bone in his face broken. The tears rolled down my face as I scheduled a flight, called friends to ask for prayers, packed my suitcase, and left for the airport.

I was met in Colorado by my daughter-in-law's father, who had arrived earlier that day from Vermont. After a big hug and mutual tears, he told me that my son was badly swollen and in need of surgery.

Hesitant to go into Steve's room, I gulped and straightened my back for courage. I hardly recognized this Sumo wrestler lying with bandaged head and closed eyes. However, my son's name was on the hospital room door, so I kissed something on him and he groaned in recognition.

What heartache! The doctor said his biggest concern in repairing Steve's face would be the amount of blood there. This youthful doctor had operated on many injuries resulting from skiing accidents, so was experienced for his young age. How blessed we were that he was there for Steve. Thank you, God!

The doctor left to sleep while I sat by Steve's bed all night. He had been frightened the night before when his throat closed after downing some Ensure through his wired-shut jaw. We learned he was lactose intolerant that night. Who knew? We were again full of gratitude for his living through one more unexpected challenge.

In the morning, I gently took hold of both his feet and visualized blood leaving his face. I aligned myself with Spirit and with all my heart and soul visualized the blood leaving his head and coming down into his body.

He was wheeled into the operating room at 7:00 AM and after lovingly kissing him, I went into the chapel. There I prayed, sent Steve and the doctor energy and visualized for hours, continuing to tell the blood to leave the facial area. Lunchtime came and went without any news from the operating room.

Dinnertime came and went. After thirteen hours, a weary doctor came in to tell me he had been able to repair the entire face because there had been very little blood there!

Tears ran down my face as I thanked God and my spirit guides for their presence and answered prayer. My ex-husband later came to relieve me of the night shift and I, feeling thankful, finally slept.

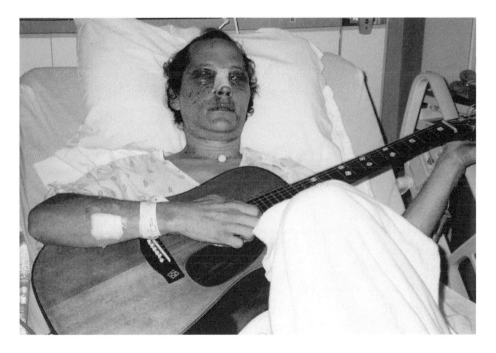

Steve never needed another operation on his face, even though it took months for his jaw to heal so he could eat solid food. His body took longer, and he was afraid he would never be the carpenter he had been before the accident. But when he finally felt like he was really going to recover his old self, he built a beautiful table as a special gift of gratitude to his doctor.

Yesterday this photo card arrived announcing the high school graduation of the baby girl born as her dad fought for his life. My heart was full of gratitude for her life and future promise.

Later in the day, I found myself re-reading Steve's journal account of a semester in India his senior year at the College of the Atlantic in Bar Harbor, Maine. It ends with this glimpse into his heart:

"While waiting outside the airport in Delhi, a small Indian boy approaches. Not begging, just looking. He sees a flute sticking out of my handbag. Soon after, a police officer asks how much it cost me and where it came from.

'Ten rupees,' I say. 'From Varanasi.'

He pointed out the boy and says how he knew this particular boy was special. Quickly we resolve the issue. The officer gives me ten rupees and the flute is the boy's. So excited, I board my plane. The engines roar, my heart roars, and we're off toward home."

Years later, I bought a handmade wooden flute from a Native American here in Arizona, and gave it to Steve. Because of his kind heart, there is flute music in Colorado as well as in India.

Breast Cancer Strikes My Daughter

My daughter Joedy called from her home in Honolulu to say she had been diagnosed with breast cancer and required surgery. My heart sank. How could this be? No one in our family had ever had breast cancer, and Joedy was a young mother.

With heart fluttering and many prayerful intentions set, I made plane reservations to be with her for whatever she needed. I looked forward to giving her the best that I could offer, my touch of healing energy.

She had surgery and faced four months of chemotherapy treatments. It was painful to see my once vibrant, active daughter with beautiful page-boy length hair, now with her drained, pale face and bald head. My eight-year-old granddaughter insisted that her mother wear a hat when she had a playmate in the house.

I was there to cook until Joedy could stand the smell of food again. So I cooked for her family, flew home for a few days to cook for my husband, and then started the cycle over again.

The day came when I was ready to give her an energy treatment. My lawyer daughter reluctantly agreed, probably because I was so eager to do this, not because she believed it would matter. I placed my hands on her prone body and mentally began the process of directing love and Divine energy to wherever it was needed.

Horrors... my nose began to run. What to do? My energy teacher, Rosalyn Bruyere, had said not to break physical contact when giving a treatment. But my daughter was freaked out by my dripping nose and asked me to please stop the treatment and forget about future energy sessions.

I was crushed, as I knew Divine energy, through me, would be healing and I had failed because of a drippy nose. This was not the plan. Perhaps not as I had imagined, but I vowed to always carry a Kleenex, and honored her wishes. Perhaps Joedy had received love through my meals and presence during this scary time.

Happily, the important five-year period with no cancer recurrence has passed, and we have our miracle. Perhaps all it took that time was a doctor's skill, a mother's love, an awareness that miracles do not come as we pray and expect them to... and a patient's belief in her doctor's treatment.

As for me, this mother and grandmother is grateful for the prayers of others and feels blessed for her daughter's recovery. My growth was in realizing that love (Spirit) is the healer. My hands, drippy nose and disappointment were nowhere near as powerful as LOVE. My job was to be in alignment with that power.

I don't know that I believe in the supernatural,
but I do believe in miracles,
and our time together was filled with events
of magical unlikelihood.

John Perry Barlow
American poet and essayist

A Fibroid and a Baby

Our youngest grandchild, age eleven at the time of publication, nearly wasn't. Daughter Laurie was in her early forties and had never been pregnant. Of all the children, she was the one who was a natural with kids and so wanted a partner who would share the dream of a child with her. She was in a relationship with Joe, who was committed to her, but not sure if he was too old to raise a child and was afraid he had missed that opportunity.

I got a telephone call on a Sunday afternoon from Laurie, telling me that while visiting her doctor on Friday, she was advised to schedule surgery to have several fibroid tumors removed from her uterus. The biggest concern was regarding a pesky, large fibroid situated on the wall of her uterus, far away from the incision point. My heart sank down to my toes and I sent a quick prayer to Spirit that the surgery would not ruin her dream of having children.

The date was set and I flew to Minnesota to be with them. Joe and I kissed this young woman in a green gown with the usual hairnet on her hair around her worried face. Believing in co-creation, I went immediately to the chapel, where I visualized that worrisome fibroid moving close to the incision point. I called upon all her guides and mine to assist.

Joe came scurrying in to take me up to Laurie's room. He said the surgery was over and the doctor would be in shortly to talk to us. I KNEW it would be good news.

Laurie looked groggy, but awake when she was wheeled in, and Joe and I kissed her and sat down to await the news.

In came a smiling doctor who announced that she was amazed to find that pesky fibroid right under her knife at the point of incision and that it was easily removed. She added gently with a smile, "Laurie, you should be able to carry a child."

I started to tell the doctor about visualization, but glanced at Laurie who was silently making that mouth-zipping motion. I got the message.

Joe and I thanked the doctor, and months later I sobbed with joy with the news of Laurie's pregnancy. As much as I believe we are co-creators with God, I admit to being awed when stuff like this happens.

I know that when we move forward with belief in who we are, and in the power we have that was also in Jesus Christ, miracles are ordinary happenings.

I find joy in the stories of how this little girl dresses for Sunday school, arrives at the church in time to pull the long rope that hangs in the bell tower. She loves to hear it summon people to service on Sunday mornings in Minnesota. Then she goes to either her piano lesson or PRIVATE skating lessons (because of her talent). She is much loved by the family, her friends and really all who come into her loving energy. A co-creative gift that began that day in the hospital years before.

Greensburg Home

My new husband's best friend was minister of a Presbyterian church in the Pennsylvania town where he lived and worked. However, one day Bob sighed and told John that the church committee, working to build a nursing home in the area, was stuck with financial challenges and organizational disputes. Would he agree to be on the committee? John told me his inner feeling was one of excitement and a joyous knowing that this was his to do.

I'll skip the details and tell you that this home was built and has been a model for other retirement homes in Pennsylvania.

There were times when John negotiated with bankers by himself and reported the result to a much smaller committee than had originally been set up. I was even recruited to fly to another state and in one day made over two-hundred decorating decisions that allowed the home to feel homey and lovely to its residents. A director was hired, again the result of my participation on the Personnel Committee, and John's and my job was done. I am proud that my husband and I pooled our talents and responded to guidance to co-create the Greenburg Home.

We walked away, and only the lawyer who had been on the original small committee remembers our involvement those thirty-five years ago.

We live many states away now and there is no contact or need for us anymore. We almost forgot that part of our lives, but the FEELING at the time, that we were part of the Creator's plan, persists.

When did you have a very strong feeling about something in your life, and does the memory of that feeling remain?

How important to seek guidance in what we are to do in life with the <u>feeling</u> that it is ours to do.

Sometimes the best thing that you can do
is not think, not wonder, not imagine, not obsess.
Just breathe and have faith...
because miracles do happen.

Coincidental Meeting?

Granddaughter Marika.

My daughter and family came to Arizona from Hawaii for the week after Christmas. Eager to show them Watson Lake, a unique lake totally surrounded by beautiful rocky formations, we drove over, parked, and they gazed in wonder at the beauty. They took off on a path leading down to the water's edge while I stayed at the top, opened my camera and took a few photos.

Soon I encountered a young family coming up from the lake. The woman had a large Canon camera and was composing a shot with her husband who was holding their two-year-old son. I wandered over and offered to take a picture of the three of them, to which they eagerly accepted. We started talking and I discovered that they had just returned from Chile where his family still lived. I told them about my trip to Chile a few years earlier and we relaxed in the beautiful setting here in Prescott.

Finding out that he was an architect with a Scottsdale firm, I told him about my granddaughter, Marika, a senior architecture student in Georgia and an intern with a different Scottsdale firm. He was impressed with what he heard, pulled out a card and encouraged me to have her contact him.

They were the nicest folks and I was almost sorry to see my family climbing up to where we were standing and the conversation ended.

I phoned Marika, already back at college, and she looked up his firm on her computer while we talked. With excitement she commented that the firm was just what she had been thinking would be the next step in her internship process. As she thanked me for giving her his contact information, I once again thanked guidance for the opportunity for a miracle moment.

In wilderness I sense the miracle of life.
and behind it our scientific accomplishments fade to trivia.
Charles Lindbergh

Lost and Found

On this day John drove to a familiar car shop to have a tracking device put in his car. Pleased with the thought of a savings in our insurance, he offered to drive my car to the same garage to have a similar tracking device installed.

The next day he left the house, only this time he couldn't find the shop. He pulled over to the side of the road, trembling with panic.

What was wrong? He'd gone to this garage for years, and again just yesterday. He had to get home. He had to stop shaking.

He finally arrived home and sat alone in his office. He was filled with negativity and wouldn't talk to me about what had happened. He looked at the phone book for the shop's address and then a city map. Still, he couldn't remember or locate this garage.

He had never had anything like this happen before. Still shaking he said, "I allow you, Spirit, my highest self, to express yourself through me."

As he sat praying, a thought drifted into his mind: "What about trapped emotions?"

Through his study of Dr. Bradley Nelson's work, John knew trapped emotions could lead to physical challenges. He had found one of Dr. Nelson's therapists in a nearby community who used muscle testing to know where and when to ask the patient to release these stuck emotions. John had already had many weekly telephone sessions with her working on anger and fear issues from his past. But how could trapped emotions be linked to what happened today?

Then he thought of his recent balance problems. He had become more wobbly these days and had even fallen flat on his back in the bathroom and passed out. There was talk with his doctor of a possible inner ear condition and, perhaps, yet another test.

With a new resolve, he came out of his office, told me what had happened and asked if I would lead him in my car to the garage.

When we returned home, he was ready for his weekly telephone session. John told her that he was mostly interested in having her work on his balance. She was surprised, as he had not mentioned that was a problem before, but his balance calibrated at an eight on a ten-point scale, higher than any remaining issues.

She worked on balance for thirty minutes, reducing it to a six, and then more... finally getting it to zero. He walked around the room and told her he was definitely improved.

John told me that he was convinced he had the memory episode and panic in order to bring balance to the fore and get it reduced. Since then, his balance has been greatly restored and he has had no further episodes of being lost.

Is this an example that out of a challenge, guidance happens and extraordinary things occur? It is important to remember that John had set the intention to allow Spirit to guide him.

I believe that we have to set an intention for what we co-create in our lives. Guidance does not just come out of the blue. We have to align ourselves with Spirit and what we have asked to come into our lives. Being congruent with Spirit is our task. Not remaining lost is our reward.

Miracles do not, in fact, break the laws of nature.
Miracles are a retelling in small letters of the very same story which is written across the whole world in letters too large for some of us to see.

C.S. Lewis

The Gift of Reading

My husband's parents came from Greece to America and settled in a small town in West Virginia. John never remembered being read to... life was just too busy for his parents trying to succeed in their new country. In school, while he was a whiz at math, the kids and teachers made fun of his inadequate attempts at reading.

When I married John, he had been able to mostly overcome this challenge. He had graduated from West Virginia University, and owned his own company. I was sad that he didn't read for pleasure as I loved to do. His reading was more like studying. He read a sentence more than once, underlined words and his book choices were more for learning the subject matter than for enjoyment. He envied my ability to read for pleasure.

When our grandchildren come for overnights, a bedtime story from me is a must. My husband can't believe that I've really read all the books in our house. I stoutly defend myself and say that of course I've read almost all of them, and the others are ones I've bought that I look forward to reading when I have time. There are bookcases in almost every room. John was amazed to learn that a granddaughter had read all the Harry Potter books by age twelve.

I soon noticed that at home, where he didn't have a secretary, he asked me to edit his correspondence. Letters were reversed, the numbers three and five were often mixed up and there were other signs that indicated dyslexia. He took a speed-reading class, but it didn't help.

When his 14-year-old son came to live with us, I was amazed that this bright young man had so much difficulty with a list of ten spelling words. When he took a phone message and left a note, it was like deciphering a foreign language. We had him tutored and he later graduated from law school. He even writes political speeches for important candidates now.

I was proud that a niece asked John to be the master of ceremonies at her wedding reception; however, she waited to ask him that day, just before the ceremony. She was marrying an Italian young man with a difficult last name. I guess I shouldn't have been surprised when the time came to introduce this newly married couple to the gathered crowd, John mispronounced that unfamiliar written name. He still remembers his embarrassment.

Years later we retired and moved to Prescott, Arizona. There we met a woman from our church whose work was brain integration. She had folks of all ages come for a weekly session to help them with their reading skills. Often she was booked for months ahead, and we were proud to know her and of her work in helping so many.

Recently John came into the kitchen with a big grin on his face. He was holding a letter that had arrived in the mail from an insurance company. It asked if he wanted to cash in the life insurance policy that his mom had taken out on him when he was a young boy. She had paid fifty cents a month for years and the policy had been paid up for awhile. It was worth $1,200. If held until his death, it would only be worth a hundred dollars more.

"For heaven's sake, cash it in and get something nice for yourself," I said.

"If you think I should, I'll cash it and put it in our account," was his reply.

"No way," I replied. "Your mother sacrificed for years so that she could do something good for you."

Then I thought of the brain integration our friend did. The cost was just about what the policy was worth.

"Reading for pleasure is the biggest regret in your life," I said. "I can't think of a gift that would both please your mother and mean something special to you." Johnny had clearly been his mother's favorite, and she always regretted not being able to help him more. But most of the time, Greek was spoken at home and her English was broken and barely understandable.

Now a year later, our evenings are spent reading... both of us. And he has a stack of books waiting to be devoured. What a gift, from a mom who had passed away years ago, to her grateful son! I'd call his decision, and result of how to use the money, a wonderful miracle.

John and his mother at the former family home in Greece.

Our Bunny Breeder Granddaughter

My granddaughter, Lauren, grew up with Bunny. Since her dad was allergic to dogs and cats, the normal household pets, her mother suggested bunnies. When I went to their house, I was amazed that my daughter had created a bunny complex in one half of the dining room. Inside the wire cage was a water-drinking system, straw to cushion Bunny's bed, a step to climb up on to see better the folks in the house, and plenty of room for my granddaughter to get into the cage to play with and cuddle her Bunny.

Each year when I visited, of course, I greeted Bunny, petted her creamy, soft hair and loved connecting to her big piercing eyes.

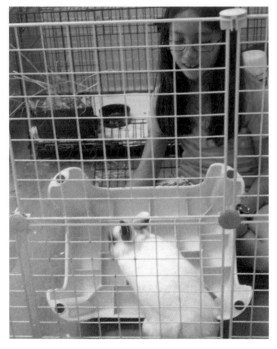

Lauren had to be reminded to sweep out Bunny's habitat, but she accepted this chore as hers to do with few complaints. Her dad would occasionally lament that the cage took up lots of room in the house, the smell sometimes 'got to him,' and he yearned for the day when his child would be off to college and perhaps the bunny would have outlived its purpose.

For purpose Bunny had. Just as I was raised by two scientific parents and yearned for a more 'feeling' environment, Lauren was raised by a lawyer and a science teacher. Perhaps that was what bonded us. Her mother once told me that my granddaughter 'adored' me. And Bunny gave her much opportunity to be loving.

When Lauren was a teen, the family, which included her older brother, Chris, went with others to Italy to celebrate my 75th birthday. This particular evening we went into town for dinner.

Looking at the menu, my grandson spied a dish he had never tried... cooked rabbit. He managed to point to it on the menu, thus not risking a reaction from his kid sister. Fortunately, Lauren's and my dinners were brought out first and we were advised to dig in while the food was hot, and we did.

So, when the waitress arrived and announced that she had a rabbit dish, Lauren gasped, turned white and no longer could eat a bite. Her mother spoke up and announced that Chris could certainly 'try' a new dish if he wanted. I saw the horror on Lauren's face. She had often told me that when she grew up she wanted to be a bunny breeder since she loved them so. She just couldn't deal with her brother's action.

Noticing that a flea market was set up in the square outside the restaurant, I proposed that Lauren and I leave the table. Outside I suggested to this teenager — who made earrings for her local school's fund raisers — that we look at the booths and each choose a pair of earrings to buy to remember our trip to Italy.

There were many lovely pairs to consider, but we finally made our choices just before the rest of the family left the restaurant, full and happy with their dinners eaten.

Lauren and I will always remember walking around the market, and we have our earrings to remind us of a special evening together. Her mother was grateful the nice evening hadn't been ruined.

Lauren is now in college, much more confident. And I continue to believe that love is the most powerful force in our lives and can heal anything. It surely deepened and broadened good feelings in the family that evening in Italy.

The Definition of Importance

Ever hear the old saying, "The apple doesn't fall far from the tree?"

Well, it's a common saying in our family to refer to those things that children do that reflect the parents' values and behaviors. I woke up thinking of a grandson's recent behavior.

Our son drove up from Phoenix to visit, bringing our 16-year-old grandson and his best friend. After the usual greetings and news of recent sports exploits (his basketball team won the state championship), our grandson asked if there was anything he could do to help us. We were in the backyard and I pointed to a water fountain that my husband had made for me years before out of stones. Years of neglect had allowed mud to fill in the pond area along with a dead tadpole or two floating around. I said that I wanted it cleaned up before Grandad's 90th birthday party this summer in the backyard.

Five minutes later, I was startled to see both boys with tools from the garage, gloves on hands, and a hose pulled over to go into action. Shortly afterward... DONE! They had big smiles on their faces as I exclaimed in joy and gratitude.

I thought of our son who wowed the Greek relatives when we traveled there a summer or two, with the fact that he had been a state senator. This attorney son is now in business with the owner of two major sports teams (you would recognize the name), along with other lucrative ventures.

But what I love to hear about is how he spent Easter Sunday in the nursery of his church, taking care of infants. He tells me that next year he will take care of the one-year-olds, the two-year-olds next, and so on. That way he will have a relationship with these kids when they become teens. He has been committed to cleaning toilets at the church once a month for years now. Did I mention that he also graduated with a degree from the Fuller Theological Seminary a year ago? We have gone to a mega-church to hear several talks of his.

We all have choices as to what we do that our children notice. I have been told that this son is 'an important man.' I wonder if they realize what is behind my proud smile.

It's What Families Do

Deciding that it is time to give my adult children the important papers I have kept while they were away at various colleges, living in too small first apartments, busy with babies, and then, oh, so involved with their lives. I was looking for a child's birth certificate in a safety deposit box on the floor of my clothes closet when I came upon a treasure.

The treasure was a letter my mother had written Dad when she was in Maryland helping my grandmother clear out the family farmhouse. I remember that at that time, Grandmother was in her eighties and had finally agreed to spend half of the year with my uncle, who lived in California, and the other half with Mother, who lived in Ohio. The farmhouse had sold, so had to be cleaned out.

"Daddy, my darling," her letter began. "There are things I like better than getting up in the early morning in an unheated house with the only bathroom an outhouse down a path beside the chicken coop. I've been wishing for my long-sleeved nightgown, but I'm an old softie compared to Mother. She gets up without complaining and comes downstairs to build a fire."

My grandmother had a master's degree from Columbia University in New York and had taught at the University of Indiana. But when my grandfather got cancer, she moved to the less expensive country-side. They raised chickens, went antiquing, he painted oils, and she helped the neighbors with their tax returns or sewed doll clothes.

But the letter goes on: "Today is her 84th birthday and I'm afraid it will be spent, as all other previous days, looking over 'stuff,' finding reminders of life long passed, giving away or burning up dreams and hopes once held that can no longer be realized."

My mind stopped for a minute thinking of dreams never realized. It brought me back to a box full of clippings my mother kept in a drawer, waiting for when she could write that book — that was never written. Perhaps including this letter in my book will fulfill that unmet dream of hers.

"Elizabeth seems to be normal for her," she continued with the letter. My husband and I lived in Baltimore, thirty miles from the farmhouse with our four children under six years of age.

"Joedy has a cold, Laurie and Steve are probably catching it. The heat in their almost completed house seems to be okay, but Joe (my first husband) needs to get a door hung between the kitchen and the garage... has a blanket hung there now. Steve spilled a bottle of Crème de Menthe and drank some. So things sound normal.

"I hope you are all right. Thank you for your patience in putting up with these long periods of my being away. All my love, Me, your wilderness wife (no newspaper, no television, no contact with the world outside... thank goodness for the mailman!)."

I was reminded of my own son-in-law's comment when I thanked him recently for his patience in coming from the warm, blue skies of Honolulu to our snow-covered Prescott, Arizona, while my daughter started helping me clear out treasures kept under the beds and in the tops of closets. His words were, "It's what families do."

One of his students asked Buddha. Are you the messiah? No. answered Buddha.
Then are you a healer? No. Buddha replied.
Then are you a teacher? The student persisted. No. I am not a teacher.
Then what are you? Asked the student. exasperated.
I am awake. Buddha replied.

Chapter 5:
Healing Stories

Help, I'm on the Ceiling
Sid Wolf
Are You Listening?
My Heart Opening That Changed Everything
Vancouver Vibes
Sacred Healing
Bedside Visitor
What Are the Chances?
Two Cemetery Stories
Sandra's Alzheimer Story
The Rest of the Real Estate Rape Story

Help! I'm on the Ceiling

The vice principal of the high school barged into my counseling office with a girl dressed like a gypsy, a turban on her head and a scary expression stating, "She says she's on the ceiling and can't get down. Can you help?"

Out of my mouth came these words, addressed to the girl, "Of course, I can help you, come on in and sit down."

I remember feeling that there was no doubt that this would occur. The vice principle closed the door with a relieved look on her face and Gloria and I started to talk. I listened to her account of a stressful encounter with the school librarian, helped her through that challenge and no more needed to be said about the ceiling.

This appears, on the surface, to be a miracle for this high school girl... but it's not. The miracle was mine.

It was one of those times when I made a connection with Spirit. I just knew and I trusted that feeling of inner guidance. I JUST KNEW.

Those times aren't planned, easily explained or common. When we have them, do we recognize the alignment with Universal creator that we have?

I'll never forget the strong inner feeling that I could do whatever was needed to get her down off the ceiling.

```
        ...when you are convinced that all the exits are
     blocked, either you take to believing in miracles
          or you stand still like the hummingbird.
     The miracle is that the honey is always there,
      right under your nose, only you were too busy
             searching elsewhere to realize it.
        The worse is not death but being blind,
     blind to the fact that everything about life
             is in the nature of the miraculous.

                     Henry Miller
                   American writer
```

Sid Wolf

In 1971, I returned to school for the master's degree in guidance and counseling program at Towson University. This decision manifested the miracle of meeting Dr. Sid Wolf, who was the most influential mentor in my life.

I had scheduled an appointment in October of my final year to apply for a job in Baltimore County after graduation. I was interviewed by a woman whose father had taught my brother in Sunday school and knew my grandparents. What a coincidence... or was it the *Law of Attraction* at work?

Ester Hicks says that 'things always work out for me.' This story is an example in my life of how being in alignment makes my life 'work.'

Only weeks later, I was offered a full-time position beginning in two weeks. A counselor had accepted a special opportunity in Washington, D.C., beginning that November and the school needed a replacement. It wasn't an easy decision for me since I had four children in school and three more courses to complete at Towson. Since my husband had recently been laid off, however, the opportunity was a Godsend. Or was it a miracle?

In January of that year, Dr. Sid Wolf, after completing his doctoral studies, offered to work for two years with five of the county's several hundred counselors, nurses and school psychologists in preparation for in-service courses that he believed would significantly change the atmosphere of the schools. Dr. Wolf's research showed that the qualities *within the helping person* had the most significance toward others' change.

It wasn't the method or the technique ~ institutionalization or not ~ or the therapy length that most mattered. What was important were the ten core qualities of empathy, warmth, respect, genuineness, self-disclosure, concreteness, immediacy, confrontation, potency, and self-actualization.

Dr. Wolf's scale showed that most people functioned at Level 2, which was not helpful to a fulfilled life, and impossible in the creation of miracles.

Years later at a Legal Enforcement Alliance of America meeting in Chicago, Dr. Wolf and I presented research showing a significant positive difference in the school atmosphere when teachers and students understood and raised the level of their ten core qualities.

Our work and time together for those two years helped each of the five of us to grow in these qualities. This was an important time in my life, and I grew in consciousness as a result of my relationship with Dr. Wolf and my colleagues. Through a choice to respond to an opportunity, I was in a position to later accept a challenge to grow as a person.

The research of Dr. David Hawkins also confirms that positive qualities in a person lead to a better life. His research shows that a person with positive qualities can score above 200 on his scale of consciousness. Below 200 lie negative qualities, making co-creation of miracles and a joy-filled life impossible.

I recognized a spiritual component within Dr. Wolf, and he told me of his studies with the Lemurian Fellowship (School of Universal Philosophy) in California. He was indeed a model for the quality of self-actualization.

I, too, became a student of the Fellowship for many years. Seeking opportunities to learn and grow spiritually has been a driving inner force all my life and I believe if a person does not respond to that pull, they have nothing more to learn.

Abraham Maslow has written of the importance of a self-actualized life and says that we all grow when we are around people who have continued to learn and expand. Maslow's Hierarchy of Needs is a theory in psychology proposed in his 1943 paper, "A Theory of Human Motivation" in *Psychological Review*.

Think of the special people in your life. Would you say they are loving, caring and open people who are in alignment with Divine qualities?

Life is not measured
by the number of breaths
we take, but by the moments
that take our breath away.

Maya Angelou

Are You Listening?

At the completion of my own training, I worked with Dr. Wolf in training Baltimore County employees communication skills to enable them to be in alignment with their ten core qualities and, therefore, raise the positive atmosphere in the schools and various county facilities.

Dr. Wolf and our team had a contract to facilitate Baltimore County's police in listening, communication skills and the ten core qualities. As homework one week, we challenged the men to really listen to people's needs, then come back and report their experiences.

The men left, grumbling with this assignment. However, the next week a desk sergeant confessed that he had been annoyed every Saturday night, week after week, by a drunken old woman. She muttered to herself as she sat on the bench beneath his high desk.

On that particular Saturday night, he leaned over, focusing his eyes in the most caring way possible, all the while inwardly expecting to have a great failure to report to class.

Through anguished sobs, the woman quietly revealed that her daughter and son-in-law made her care for her retarded granddaughter all week. The girl was chained and kept in an upstairs closet. Saturday night was the woman's time off.

The sergeant put his big arms around her since he had really heard her, and then sent a team over to the house. They were stunned to find an eight-year-old girl, thin and only able to crawl like a baby.

The class was silent, perhaps reflecting on times when they had been too busy to listen to another, or too disinterested to believe anything important was being expressed.

Deep listening is compassion, and often leads to healing... even miracles.

> The miracle is not that we do this work,
> but that we are happy to do it.
>
> Blessed Teresa of Calcutta
> Albanian Roman Catholic nun and missionary

My Heart Opening that Changed Everything

I lived in the countryside outside of Baltimore when the children were young. The bookmobile was important for me and the children. One of my favorite books was *Joy's Way*, by Dr. W. Brugh Joy. Dr. Joy was a workshop leader who held retreats in California, far from Maryland and, I was sure, too expensive for a young mother of four.

The day came when the children had grown and my husband and I moved to Arizona. Shortly after moving, I met Maria Elaina Darby in Phoenix who suggested that I consider attending a heart opening workshop, given by her associate, Brugh Joy. And, no, not in California but just up the road in Paulden, Arizona. I went.

Toward the end of the workshop, we were told to dress in white, and one by one become the center of the group's attention. When my turn came to lie on the massage table, the others gathered around and flooded me with their touches of energy and love. Brugh challenged me to open my heart as it had never been opened before.

I was in a deep meditative state when I left the table and the room. Challenged to follow our guidance as to where to go from there, I headed down to the outdoor pool, my favorite place at the Wilderness Lodge. As I walked the path, it seemed natural that the trees bowed, the rocks moved and the birds sang. I took my outer clothes off and floated on the surface of the heated water looking up at the sky and seeing faces in the clouds.

That experience of the altered state, when everyone in the room sent love to me, allowed me to see and feel that connection with the Divine. It opened my heart wider and raised my consciousness to a new depth of understanding... of life... of everything.

Focused intention of love. Dr. David Hawkins says Love is the most powerful energy in the Universe – that Love heals. Love created the Universe with focused intention.

It was a time of KNOWING that we are all connected by energy; that energy is in everything. I was truly in an altered state. Brugh told me later that his mother had had a similar experience of having the trees bow as she walked one day.

When I returned home from that workshop my husband could feel the expansion and increased depth of my heart and said, "I want what you have."

He signed up for the next workshop, resulting in a new richness in our relationship. He listened to his inner guidance, made a choice or, you might say, allowed a miracle to occur.

To be alive, to be able to see, to walk,
to have houses, music, paintings --
it's all a miracle.
I have adopted the technique of living life,
miracle to miracle.

Arthur Rubinstein
Polish American classical pianist

Vancouver Vibes

Several years after studying with Brugh Joy, I studied with Rosalyn Bruyere, an energy teacher who was also known for having had Barbara Brennan as a student. Both women have written influential books in their field.

This was a time in my life when I could build on my skills as an energy healer. I went to five workshops with Rosalyn in Phoenix, Santa Fe and California and she was indeed a powerful energy worker. I traveled from Prescott to Phoenix each Monday morning to do volunteer energy work with other therapists on clients from the Phoenix area.

One year, Rosalyn took fifty of us to Vancouver. We gathered in the local gym where we spent a week with the Squamish Indians in a healing workshop. There were four of us on each team.

One day a Squamish Indian woman hesitantly came over to our table. She lay down and as we stood over her, she began to cry. When we started to touch and send her energy, she sobbed loudly and Rosalyn came over to evaluate.

She told us to keep doing our work, and reassured us that the woman had no physical problems. When the session was over, the woman sat up and smiled at us. She stated that she had never let a white person touch her, and neither had anyone in her family. Generations of experiences with white people betraying them had created an energy of contact with white people that was truly negative and prevented her from positive feelings. She said that she felt healed of this fear during our session with her.

When she got down off the table, she turned to me and asked how she could continue with her growth. Her lifelong fear of white people had kept her from trusting and kept her from having relationships in her life. I suggested that she keep a journal and write her feelings out and meditate on them. Startled, she looked at me and asked how I knew that she was a writer. My honest answer was that I just KNEW.

Was it guidance or another ordinary miracle of listening to what we call intuition?

I have recently read Dr. Bradley Nelson's book, *The Emotion Code*, in which he details the process of removing ages-old emotions that have blocked our growth. When we do not deal with our fears, it limits us — keeps us from opportunities to love.

That woman had generations of bad vibes that manifested in fear from whites, and they were released that day. Our team was blessed to have had the chief's daughter on our table. Out of this chance assignment, we were invited to go to the chief's house for dinner the

last night in Vancouver. There we saw his incredible art work and met his wife, a Hungarian princess! What a miraculous evening, another blending of art and compassion in my life's journey.

I bought a piece of glass that the Chief had made, as a reminder of this time. When a granddaughter admired it, I was joy-filled to know that the loving energy within would go to her in my will!

To find your own piece of Vancouver art, go to my Bibliography at the back of this book for the website and contact information of Sky Spirit Studio.

Love is the great miracle cure.
Loving ourselves works miracles in our lives.

Louise L. Hay

Sacred Healing

Our Prescott minister attended a Unity conference where a fellow pastor spoke about energy healing. I had met with our minister many times seeking such an opportunity to offer this at our church. But he was concerned about liability issues.

The conference pastor mentioned that he could insure any church that had its practitioners trained by him, so we scheduled his coming. We were trained and began holding weekly Wednesday Prayer and Energy Healing services.

Following a session one woman was amazed to find that she no longer had macular degeneration. A man told of his brain tumor reduction, another woman of being present at her friend's transition in another state. We knew that whenever the person on the receiving end of energy transmission opened his or her heart, and aligned with Spirit, miracles could happen.

And as Rosalyn Bruyere often said in her training sessions, "Give a healing, get a healing." So the practitioners benefited as well.

We are the miracle of force and matter
making itself over into imagination and will.
Incredible.
The life force experimenting with forms.
You for one. Me for another.
The universe has shouted itself alive.
We are one of the shouts.

Ray Bradbury
American fantasy, science fiction, horror and mystery author

Bedside Visitor

She jumped up onto the massage table, one of eight people signed up for a Sacred Healing Meditation experience. We facilitators never knew why the person had come or what would unfold each evening.

Reverend Scott Sherman had trained ten of us, and we meditated in the Sanctuary upstairs before going down to the library where the tables had been set up. Most of the people who came for this 30-minute session, heard a soothing tape recording while a practitioner gave light touch to open the chakras and relieve pain. Sometimes it was physical, sometimes emotional.

I stood next to the woman on the table this particular night, waiting for the soothing voice of Rev. Sherman to begin on the tape. Her eyes were closed; we had not exchanged any words, just loving smiles. We did not seek to know what in particular brought each person to the table, but encouraged them to clear their minds and get into an attitude of openness and love.

As the music began, I felt an unusual and unexpected chill and noticed that her face was quite pale and immobile. I thought that she looked like death.

Whoa! I struggled to concentrate on love. As I proceeded to clear her chakras, using my hands to feel any energy imbalances, she didn't seem present. It was as if she had left her body there on the table and was somewhere else. Again, I focused on loving her and asking Spirit to work through me to do whatever this woman needed.

She still didn't move a muscle. Usually the person receiving this loving treatment will twitch, move a hand or cough. For the entire half hour, she made no movement at all. I thought she must be so deeply relaxed that I wondered what she was feeling, if anything. I returned to focusing on sending love.

Soon I heard the ending words and directions in the recording. She was to place her left hand on her stomach and her right hand on her heart, but still she didn't move. The tape recording stopped, and the other practitioners gently helped their clients up to a sitting position and offered them the customary drink of water. There were soft mutterings in the room as the 'receivers' spoke of their experience to the 'givers' who were standing beside the tables. My eyes could see that all the others were in the process of getting off their tables and looking for their shoes. Not my woman. She was still as could be. I placed my hands on her, hoping for some response. Suddenly her eyes opened and color returned to her face.

Her eyes were as wide as mine as she began to talk. "My best friend is dying in a hospital in another state. When the music began, I was standing at her bedside. I felt so much love leave my body and surround her. It was wonderful to be there. She seemed to be at peace as I stood there and stroked her hand."

I offered her a cup of water and was amazed that I had sensed her leaving her body for awhile. She rose from the table, gave me a hug and thanked me for facilitating this visit with her friend. I commented that those of us in an energy healing practice offer love and our willingness to be vehicles for Spirit. She put on her coat and left. I drove home, marveling at this evening's occurrence.

In the morning, I received a phone call from the woman.

"Elizabeth," she began in a hushed voice. "I just got word that my Colorado friend passed away last night at peace, and shortly after the time of our session on the table here in Arizona."

We both gave thanks for the bedside visit. I marveled at the miracle that had occurred in the energy of love that evening.

What Are the Chances?

My friend was in her office at one of the rental properties she managed when she was puzzled by loud shouting outside. Looking out the door, she saw a retired couple who had been tenants ever since she and her husband had become property managers for the units.

The wife seldom spoke except for a soft mumbling to herself, and her husband usually looked saddened by the effects of Alzheimer's in his wife.

But here they were, along with two new renters, crying and yelling for joy. It seems the new female resident was Cherokee and recognized that the older woman's mumbling was in the Cherokee language and started talking to her.

The older woman's husband later learned that his wife was one-sixteenth Cherokee and had spoken the language at home as a child. A smile broke over his wife's face, and for a short time there was a beautiful connection between the two women, and then the husband. A tear made its way down his cheek as he realized his wife was actually speaking Cherokee and was not as lost in an Alzheimer's fog as he had believed.

Soon after, this friend had a miracle of her own: Unexpected seed money in a pension account she thought she had sold years ago to finance her graduate studies, had been left to grow for forty-seven years. It was now available to provide lifelong income. My friend said she finally understood the term 'God-smacked!' For years she had been concerned about having enough retirement savings, and all the while God was quietly working in the background, providing for her even when she didn't know it.

Even miracles take a little time.

The Fairy Godmother
A fairy with magical powers who acts as a mentor
or parent to someone

Two Cemetery Stories

My friend, Sue, told me about a time when she left Baltimore for Pittsburgh for a reunion with former Carnegie Mellon classmates. They had graduated about sixty years ago and had maintained their friendships for all this time.

Their Pittsburgh hostess took them to a scrubby, old hillside cemetery, and as she slowly drove along, challenged them to look out the window for something unusual. No one saw anything on the first pass, so she hinted that they might find a stone saying Warhol.

My friend exclaimed, "Look, there in front of a large stone are two Campbell's tomato soup cans."

Getting out of the car, they saw Andy Warhol's small grave in front of his parent's larger stone. There was a small plastic file that was slipped beside the cans with a notepad and pencils containing instructions to write the reason for visiting the grave as this person visited daily and wanted to know why others came. Unfortunately, not many people had responded, maybe not even remembering Andy Warhol.

Sue wrote that she and her colleagues were graduates of Andy Warhol's college, were having a reunion weekend, and she was honored to pay tribute to the famous artist's gravesite.

Several weeks later, the Pittsburgh hostess took others to the grave and she noticed that the note left by my friend was gone.

Why was my friend the only one who left a note? Perhaps that appreciation in her heart of Andy Warhol's artistic contribution touched the soul of the one who left the paper and pencils, and enriched her Spirit.

That story reminded me of a visit I had made several years before to a run-down, crowded cemetery in Prague, where the remains of hundreds of Jews from World War Two were buried.

There were no names, as no one knew who they had been, but we walked around the broken stones and prayed for the peace of those buried there. We honored their lives with our hearts.

These occurrences connect us in important ways and contribute to positive, loving energy in our world. Caring for the gifts of Andy Warhol and praying for those who may have been forgotten in a broken down cemetery, is a way of honoring all life. All life matters.

Miracles are the natural way of the Universe
— our only job is to move our doubting minds
out of the way.

Jonathon Lockwood Huie
Photojournalist, author, trainer, personal coach, speaker,
and creator of *Inspirational Thoughts and Encouraging Quotes*

Sandra's Alzheimer's Story

One of my dearest friends lives on the East coast, across the country from Arizona. That long distance is especially hard for me because we had raised our young children, were neighbors and members of the same church community. I ache for her as she has been diagnosed with early onset Alzheimer's. My dad died of complications from Alzheimer's so I know first-hand how the deterioration of the mind and then the body of a loved one is increasingly difficult to watch.

A few years ago, my friend's husband offered to support the two of us to attend a weekend seminar with Barbara Marx Hubbard, expanding and evolving our consciousness, so our lives have more purpose. Gratefully, we joined twenty others, all focusing on how we could contribute at this point in our lives. Many of them stood to share their dreams and to get feedback as to how to proceed.

I wondered if my friend would understand – find something new for her own life – could she contribute – could she look forward. Much to my surprise, she stood and announced that despite having early onset Alzheimer's, she lived in a community with retired women whose husbands had had important government jobs. The women spent their time playing golf or bridge. My friend told Barbara she wanted to invite them for coffee to discuss how they could be helpful to others in their community.

Barbara asked what she would need in order to follow through with her good idea and she replied, "I'd need encouragement."

Barbara asked, "Who could do that for her?"

I stood and hugged my friend while making the commitment to send her love (frequent phone support etc., etc.).

An ordinary weekend had just become sacred.

This year she flew to Arizona to honor me on my 80th birthday. The best gift was news that her new doctor diagnosed her with vascular dementia, not Alzheimer's. Sandra had changed doctors when her former doctor started addressing his questions to Sandra's husband, not to her. In addition, she had unpleasant side effects from the Alzheimer's medication that the doctor felt she should 'accept.'

Another 'miracle' due to inner guidance, self-trust and the energy of love.

Life is a miracle. You are a unique expression of this purposeful miracle. Think of how great that makes you. Live big!
You are not here to dwell within the basement of your potentiality.

Dr. Steve Maraboli

The Rest of the Real Estate Rape Story

Those of you who have read my book, *A Common Thread*, read of Linda and the real estate rapist (*Gift of the Real Estate Rapist*, Page 130).

Well, Linda telephoned me on January 2 this year. I was home alone, cooking for my daughter's family who were in Phoenix on their way to Prescott later that day for a week's visit. It was a perfect time for a chat with my old friend.

She had moved to a new state, all in an attempt to escape from the scary calls from the rapist who was still in prison, but allowed a weekly telephone call. His release, after twenty years, was imminent and the parole board promised to let Linda know when he was set free.

However, her call was to see what life was bringing me, and I told her about writing this book. Just so happens, she had recently written hundreds of pages of channeled material from a non-physical. I excitedly told her about my Tuesday group and our listening to Abraham, a group of non-physicals. How special!

When Linda and I met, many years ago, we knew we would be life-long friends. It had been many years since we had connected, however, and I was excited. My editor and I had agreed to a respite from finishing this book; she because of other work pressures, and I to see if there was guidance to hold off until a new story about a miracle should be included. Guidance works that way.

We spoke of the commonality in our two new books. Both of us recognize the importance of Joy, Love, Compassion, Peace, and Grace in life. Her working title is, *Heart to Hand* (see Bibliography). Chills went through me as I recalled my energy teacher, Rosalyn Bruyere instructing me to put one of my hands on a person's heart, and then reach the other to their hand when doing healing. We shared beliefs that when our heart opens, we want to give and our energy expands to others.

Her book speaks to illnesses such as cancer and its purpose, of Alzheimer's and Down's Syndrome children and what they teach us. I can't wait until her book comes out! We agreed to talk again soon. Her non-physical guide says there are Soul Groups in life and I know I am blessed to be in hers.

Chapter 6:
Traveling the World

————————————————————————————

First Class All the Way
Going to the Last Supper
My Russian Folk Tale
Under the Tuscan Sun
Mais oui, a French Cooking School Adventure
Pick-Pocketed in Prague
Magical Night in Athens
Luck of the Chinese Girl
Delay into Hooray!

First Class All The Way

I got out of our car, kissed my husband good-bye and pulled my little black carry-on into the Phoenix Sky Harbor Airport. It was dark outside, almost 10:30 PM, and the airport was mostly deserted. Looking for the British Airways counter, I noticed a noisy crowd of people, mostly women, standing in the economy line. Recognizing that this was my place to be, I stood at the rear of the line.

"Get out of here, we a groupa!" the pushy woman in front of me shouted. Stunned, I turned around and wheeled my bag to the empty first class area. The lone employee with a snappy British Airways flight outfit motioned me forward.

"I've been kicked out of the economy line and wonder if you could check me in," I woefully exclaimed.

With a twinkle in his eye and a glance at the chattering folks in the nearby line he said, "Certainly."

Growing in nerve I mentioned that I had recently been given a press pass since I was writing travel articles, and was told that sometimes it was possible to be upgraded. I fumbled in my purse and pulled out the newly issued press pass. He explained that upgrades were assigned by the supervisor at the boarding level, but he thought this would be a fine time to separate me from the masses and be seated where they would offer me a drink! Sounded wonderful to me.

Upstairs I sat in silence, aware of the chatter going on within the 'groupa.' Just as the announcement to board came over the loud speaker system, I heard the woman from behind the check-in desk call my name. She smilingly handed me a new boarding ticket, Row 3, Seat 2 in first class.

I resisted grinning with attitude as I boarded from the short line, past the women in the 'groupa' with their negative energy.

There was a bejeweled woman sitting in Row 3, Seat 1 when I arrived. She had multiple-carat sparkling rings on every finger and diamond-drop earrings. After exchanging first names, she immediately asked my occupation.

"I'm a therapist," I ventured, expecting the usual wary look in return.

"Oh, thank heavens. I knew I could count on British Airways to honor my request for a compassionate seat mate!" This time, it seemed, I was wanted. She went on to explain that her mother lived in London and was dying. She was on her way to be with her and arrange for her memorial. I expressed sympathy and she was well into her life story when my much-needed glass of wine arrived.

I didn't get much sleep that night, but the food service was great. I listened in comfort to my seat mate, now friend. Amazingly, we were booked on the same return flight ten days later.

"I want you to sit with me on our return," she said. I hastened to explain that my ticket was for the economy section, not first class.

"No problem," was her comment, "I'll come find you and have you moved."

Ten days later, with my mind filled with memories of a wonderful Italian cooking school with my college roommate friend, I was back in the British Airways lounge. I had checked in and took my seat. I couldn't help but look around for my first class traveling companion. She was nowhere to be found. The boarding announcement came, we filed into the plane and I took my seat in Row 37, Seat 36B.

Oh well, I had had a great trip, so far, and there was no problem with the dinner served on the plane in the economy section. I read a bit and then got sleepy, so put on my dark blue eye shades and spread out into Seat 36C, dangled my feet into the aisle and closed my eyes. I hadn't gone to sleep when I felt a tickling on my feet. Peeking out from the eye shade, who should I see but my traveling friend and a flight attendant.

"Gather your belongings and follow me," said the stewardess. Soon I was seated in Row 3, Seat 2 back in first class.

"I looked for you, but didn't see you in the lounge," my friend said. "Thank heavens I recognized your hair and shape back in the plane. Now, let me tell you about Mother."

I was sorry to hear that she had made her transition, but glad that my friend had been able to clear up her business and, more importantly, see distant relatives who still lived in London. She teared up at one point and I was my compassionate self.

Suddenly, she asked if I had ever been up in the cockpit of one of these two-decker planes. Soon the flight attendant called the pilots and asked if they would like to show 'two blondes' the view. My blond hair was bottle-fed and I was suspicious that hers was too but, oh well.

Up we went and the attendant opened the door to the inner sanctum. Two middle-aged men greeted us warmly. The plane was on auto pilot and they pointed out the ice of Newfoundland below. It truly was a beautiful sight!

Soon we were suggesting favorite restaurants for their layover in Scottsdale and it was time to return to our seats. We departed with a, "Wow! Thank you very much!"

Years later I was grateful this occurred pre-9/11!

We soon landed in Phoenix and addresses were exchanged. She gave me a hug and we stood to deplane. I felt an arm on my shoulder and the flight attendant pulled me aside.

"If you ever fly British Airways again," she whispered, "tell the agent that you did the crew a favor on a flight and, if possible, to upgrade you. I would have had my hands full with that woman if you hadn't happened to be a therapist and, with the luck of the draw, seated next to her."

"Divine Order," I replied, knowing inside that I was in alignment with Universal Love.

P.S. Years later, my husband and I flew to England on British Airways. I told him that I was going to tell my story and ask for an upgrade. He was embarrassed to go up to the counter with me. I returned to our seats in the lounge and rose with him to stand in the economy line when time to board. Suddenly at the end of a litany of names, I thought I heard ours being called.

"No," he said, "it wasn't."

"Oh well, won't hurt to go check," I replied. At the counter, the employee said that we were not called as a standby and looked puzzled.

"Perhaps we are on the upgrade list," I ventured. Sure enough, he exchanged our economy seats for two business-class seats.

"So there!" I said in glee to my husband. Then grinned at the ticket-taker who had heard my unlikely, but true, tale of a flight years ago when I had been kicked out of economy into a situation where all I had to do was be myself in showing compassion. The *Law of Attraction* was truly a reality and there are times when life is truly first class!

Going to the Last Supper

My older son was teaching a summer art course in Italy, presenting an opportunity for my husband and me to travel there. I had read that Leonardo da Vinci's *The Last Supper* had been restored in Milan and I felt a pull within to see it. It had been forty years ago when this painting had made a lasting impression on me as a young student on a college trip. Viewings were always sold out so we had to be there on time.

We had a reservation at 6:15 PM on the appointed day, and we were prompt. When admitted, along with twelve Japanese tourists, we went through three small security rooms before reaching the glorious large room where *The Last Supper* was on the end wall. I stood in front of the painting, held onto the rail, and felt like I was being pulled into the painting. I was not aware of time, only of being in the energy with those at the table. I was lost in the feelings of love and devotion. I was truly there at the last supper.

Suddenly, a bell rang and my awareness focused back into the room. Everyone else was at the opposite end of the room looking at a painting of the Crucifixion. Another bell rang indicating that our fifteen minutes were up. The usher had opened a door, and I hurried to join my husband at the exit. Outside, I sat on a bench and with amazement, tried to tell him what had happened to me. I felt a vibration and a pulling into the painting that I had never experienced before, or since.

Why did I have the desire to see that piece of art in Italy when there are so many others? I had simply expected to see a beautiful painting. But instead, my experience opened me up to a deeper level of awareness of my own spiritual oneness with the Universe.

Having never experienced a feeling like this before, it was the photographer in me who took a forbidden photo to remember this 'out of the ordinary' experience.

It is a bit fuzzy, but it was my memory and inspiration to dig deeper into my interest in both art and spirituality. More importantly, I wanted to feel closer to the Divine in my life.

What was the significance for me? I believe eternity is timeless, that my energy is a part of everything, and that when I am in emotional alignment with the Universe, miracles naturally occur. I was a loving person, there was no resistances, and art lights up my soul. I had allowed a marvelous, unexpected, and new Divine experience to happen to me that day.

What connects you to your most loving self, and do you choose to be around that which stimulates the essence of who you really are?

You were born with wings...
why prefer to crawl through life?
Forget safety. Live where you fear to live.
Destroy your reputation. Be notorious

Rumi
13th-century Persian poet, jurist, Islamic scholar,
theologian, and Sufi mystic

My Russian Folk Tale

While on a cruise up the Baltic Sea to St. Petersburg, John and I were excited to learn about Russian paper mache art objects created by villagers. The sales representative came onboard our ship for that evening only and we eased our way into the gift shop along with many other passengers.

My eye immediately went to a small black box with delicate and colorful paintings. The agent explained that the artists use only one hair from an animal as their brush; they can only paint for several years as it is too delicate and taxing on their eyes. We all looked in wonder at the treasures.

Learning that each item depicted a folk tale, I asked the spokesman to tell me the story on the little black box held tightly in my hand.

"It's the story of Vasalisa and Baba Yaga, a popular Russian folk tale. I'm sorry not to have time to tell you the story as there are so many customers."

I felt drawn to buy that box, my chosen trip souvenir, and did so trusting that I would find the fairy tale sometime in the future.

Settling into our room that evening and opening the book I had taken out of the ship's library that afternoon, I turned the pages of Caroline Myss's, *Sacred Contracts*. There, on page forty-five, I was startled to read that the story of Vasalisa and Baba Yaga was an archetypal tale dating way back to pre-historic times.

Caroline wrote, "This is a story about the power of intuition. Vasalisa, and all of us, are meant to learn to rely on our inner voice, the intuitive sense of where to go and how to proceed in life, with all its dangers and demands."

Vasalisa was a young girl whose mother was dying. She gave her daughter a tiny magical doll to guide her if she ever needed help. The father remarried a wicked step-mother who sent Vasalisa into the woods to get coals to re-light the house fire. Vasalisa consulted the doll as to the way to the old witch, Baba Yaga, the keeper of the coals. The witch required Vasalisa to complete difficult or impossible tasks, which the doll completed while the girl slept. This tale symbolizes every woman's need to use her intuition, symbolized by the doll, when dealing with difficult challenges.

Caroline Myss goes on to talk about sacred contracts. They are life courses in which we are challenged to learn lessons. All of us are meant to rely on our inner voice to grow in wisdom and consciousness.

I believe we each know when we have made unwise choices for ourselves, because of the prodding of our 'inner doll.' Sometimes, we betray ourselves by being with someone or doing something not right for us and we lament, "Why me?"

Those are times we are aware of being drained of energy, and a sure sign that we are veering from our path.

We know from experience that it takes only seconds for negative feelings to get out of our bodies; then we can <u>choose</u> positive feelings and find our way back to our path. Challenging moments lead to transformative experiences. We get these moments through our own choices. Others aren't responsible for our lives – only we have the keys.

I couldn't have chosen a more meaningful folk tale, and I have long treasured this box as one of my beloved objects.

What lies before us and what lies behind us are small matters compared to what lies within us. And when you bring what is within out into the world, miracles happen.

Henry David Thoreau

All miracles are promised to faith, and what is faith except the audacity of will which does not hesitate in the darkness, but advances towards the light in spite of all ordeals, and surmounting all obstacles?

Eliphas Levi

Under the Tuscan Sun

What a perfectly sunny idea!! It was my 75th year and being of unsound mind, I decided the way to best celebrate was to invite my grown children and their kids to come to a farmhouse in Italy for a week. Seemed like a plan to me.

I asked myself, "Why go so far? And why spend so much of our retirement income?" But I didn't let those questions deter me. As we independent women do, I pursued.

I recalled being a college student at Oberlin and being invited to join my professor for an 11-week trip to Europe. He was writing a book on the harpsichord and planning to take ten students, thus enabling his way to be paid. I convinced my parents to let me take all my money out of my summer work earnings to go. There were admonitions about needing this treasure for a first apartment, or perhaps a car upon graduation.

My parents had a plan worked out for my life: go to college, get married, have children. But, I persisted. My choice of going to Oberlin College rather than the traditional family choice of a women's college had given me an expanded vision for my life, and I knew I needed a bigger pan.

The experience in Europe changed my life. Being exposed to different cultures, seeing history come alive, experiencing various ways of living, visiting art museums and parks, hearing music of the *Folies Bergere* carbaret music hall in Paris, sitting in seventy-five-cent balcony seats enchanted by the symphony and plays in London, and developing the confidence that comes with learning how to cope with different challenges and foreign metros, helped me mature.

My college roommate and good traveling buddy had shared pictures during a recent visit to her California abode and glowing reports of a farmhouse in Tuscany where she had rented and vacationed for eight years in a row, and most recently with a friend who had both adult children and young grandchildren. "It was perfect for three generations," she reported. And I started dreaming.

First one of our sons mentioned that he would like to take his boys to Europe that summer. When a daughter also said that the family would like to travel to Europe that last summer before our grandson left for college, my mind was made up. A farmhouse, really a villa, in Tuscany would be perfect for one week and then each family could go where they wanted for the second week. I would rent the house and they would be responsible for their travel expenses.

Our art professor son wrote that he would be in Todi, Italy, in Umbria, teaching for seven weeks that summer and could stay on to join us for our week. How perfectly things were shaping up! Another daughter's plans could include meeting her partner's business associates in Germany near Frankfurt and so she was on board. Sadly, two families couldn't make it but, hey, four out of six wasn't bad.

We had learned two years before, when we spent Christmas at our daughter's in Hawaii, that for each family to have a space of their own, to be flexible about the day's activities, and to gather each evening, worked well for us.

The deposit was wired and the planning began. From that point on, never has a trip gone so perfectly! It must have been Divine Order or God's birthday gift to me, or something of the sort. The planes were on time, no one got lost, no one got sick, it was beyond our fantasy, and I stayed on budget. Doesn't get much better than that!

John and I arrived early the first day in Italy. We had agreed to prepare dinner the first night, then breakfast and lunch the second day as the other families came at different times during the first afternoon.

Let me describe grocery shopping in Italy. The first morning we paid the euro required to rent a cart at a massive Costco-like store in Poggibonsi, and ventured in. It was Saturday and quite crowded. Watching the women put on plastic gloves, select fresh produce and place it in a plastic bag was the first step. After I stood in line to weigh my bag of peaches, I quickly saw that it was wise to gather all the little bags of fresh fruits and veggies in the cart and then stand in line to weigh. I had to find the photo of the item before the scale would spit out the sticker with the correct charge. I placed the sticker on the bag and weighed the next item.

Moving on to the first of three meat counters, I took a number like we do here in the States. Only the salesperson spoke Italian. When our turn came up she waved her hands – not understanding my request for Italian sausage. That was what my recipe for spaghetti called for, but there must have been six or more varieties of Italian sausage at that counter. And then there were two more counters to go. I did better at the counter where I could see packages pre-priced and weighed.

My goodness, the wines were plentiful and cheaper than water! My sweet partner was getting concerned that our overflowing cart contained more groceries than the remaining room in our little Fiat rental car could hold. "But we need milk for the kids and some eggs and butter yet," I insisted.

My goal was to get us through the first two days and then each family could buy what they needed to prepare their turn at providing dinner. We planned three nights in, and three out at restaurants. We managed to stuff the bags into the car and were on our way to the farmhouse. The weather was glorious, and we were singing with joy.

What a relief that the cleaners from the week before had begun with the kitchen so the two refrigerators were empty and waiting for us. We marveled at the well-equipped kitchen, great dishwasher and stove... even an expresso machine!

Which table and chairs to relax in with our glasses of iced tea? We chose the white iron table under the grape arbor. The leafy roof let the breezes through and our eyes feasted on the large pink hyacinths. We took in the large swimming pool, adjoining kiddie pool, and path to the tennis court beside the kitchen garden... all for our use the coming two weeks.

Refreshed and having said, "*Prego,*" to the cleaning ladies, we
ventured up the tiled steps to select our bedroom and unpack. Each
bedroom had its own lovely bath, there was an upstairs laundry, views
from all the windows and cool breezes letting us know that no air
conditioning was going to be necessary.

We couldn't wait to see the advertised garden, 'fresh tomatoes,
lettuce, carrots and herbs,' any and all for us to eat. I filled my bag
with luscious produce, glad that I hadn't bought any of the above at
the grocery store. We glanced at the tennis court near the garden and
walked back up to the house to check out the huge swimming pool.
Lots of lounge chairs, water toys for the kids and covered tables and
chairs for cards or conversation. We were sure the pool would get used
after a time of sightseeing and before dinner. It surely was, everyday.

We met some of the families from England who were housed in
two condos on the property. One of the children, Emma, told us her
parents were one of the eight couples who had bought eight acres
comprising the farmhouse buildings and fields and had it updated and
turned into these rental units. We had the main house, nearest the

pool, and with the best views. Thanks, 'Roomy,' for sharing your eight years of experience with this little piece of heaven on earth!

Each family in turn gave me a big hug with a word of thanks. A daughter-in-law said that it was more wonderful than her wildest dreams after seeing the movie, *Under the Tuscan Sun*. My husband relaxed as each family raved and enjoyed their week. We tried the recommended restaurants, went to a local lunch-time cooking class, walked in a sculpture garden — formerly a refuge for wild boar — ate gelato in San Gimignano, Siena, Lucca, and Florence.

So many miracle moments!

My heart was blessed with the warm feeling that our family had bonded more deeply and the grandchildren experienced the connection with another culture that had so changed and expanded my early life.

What did I do this morning before sitting down to write this piece? Well, nothing breeds success like success. I have been asked to research and plan next summer's sailing trip to the Greek Isles for John's two children and their half-Greek families.

Kalimera!!

Life is a series of thousands of tiny miracles.
Mike Greenberg
Television anchor, television show host,
radio show host for ESPN and ABC, and novelist

Mais ouis, A French Cooking School Adventure

My college friend and fellow cooking school junkie, Carolyn, jumped at the advertisement in the travel section of our Phoenix, Arizona's Sunday paper, and the planning began.

We had loved Lorenza de Medici's similar opportunity in Italy years before and were ready to take on the French (read about Elizabeth's Italian cooking adventure in *A Common Thread,* Page 83). After all, we both owned copies of Julia's, *Mastering the Art of French Cooking.*

Carolyn's plane from San Francisco landed at Heathrow an hour ahead of mine from Phoenix. My plane arrived three hours later than scheduled, and I was worried about finding my way to the departure-to-France terminal in time. My heart jumped with hope as I heard the flight attendant call my name and ask me to come to the front of the plane and deplane first.

"You will be met by an airline representative at the foot of the stairway who will take you to the connecting terminal."

I gave a silent prayer of thanks to the gods who kept track of connections. The special van wound its way underneath roadways and runways, and I was pointed to an underground doorway and escalator.

There I was greeted by a security attendant who put my tote through the X-ray and then sent me on my way. Around the next bend I spied my friend, Carolyn, anxiously looking in my direction.

"I saw that your plane was delayed and worried that you wouldn't make our flight."

Telling her about the connections gods at Heathrow, we hugged and made our way to the departure gate for Nice, France. We had booked a hotel for our evening in Nice, since it was too late to pick up our rental car and besides, we were tired from the trip across the pond.

Carolyn's bag arrived on the conveyor, but not mine. This trip was not beginning as I had expected! At the customer service counter, I was handed a plastic bag with a toothbrush, paste, comb, and tee-shirt, along with the explanation that my bag would surely arrive on the next flight from Heathrow.

In the meantime, we went to the hotel, checked in and boarded the shuttle to the Mediterranean with its seafood restaurants along the beach promenade. Ah, nothing like the smell of sea water, the sight of sailing vessels and the smells of fresh fish cooking. A table with a view, a glass of wine and we had arrived!

Arriving back at the airport the next morning, we started with the car rental agency. "Sorry, we do not have the economy size car you had reserved, but we can upgrade you to a nice van." Not happy about a large car to drive on the narrow country roads, we were nevertheless anxious for something with wheels, and signed the agreement.

Expecting that my bag had arrived on one of the evening flights, Carolyn circled the airport while I ran in to claim my familiar red bag.

"Your bag has not arrived yet," were the unexpected words out of the customer service representative's mouth as he sadly shook his head. "No big black bag with your name on it has arrived from Heathrow."

"No, my bag is red, not black and it is carry-on size," I exclaimed in frustration to the baggage man who had been called to verify the sad news. I wondered why they make you fill our long forms if they don't read the most important facts: the color and size of your bag.

With the corrected information, the baggage attendant departed for a locked room and shortly appeared down the corridor pulling a familiar red bag. I breathed a sigh of relief, rolled the suitcase out to the curb, and Carolyn and I headed out of Nice. We stopped to visit St. Paul de Vence before getting on the highway toward Velázquez and the House with Blue Shutters, which was to be our home for the next five days for the sight-seeing leg of our journey before attending the cooking school. We chose a little village near towns that had special museums, beautiful vistas, local markets, and romantic names like Avignon, Arles, Les Baux, and Roussillon.

We drove our big van up the hilly road to Velázquez, carefully maneuvered around the fountain in the center of the village, with stone walls guarding the village dwellings, and asked the lone person walking on the street for directions to the House with Blue Shutters. You would think that the shutters would have identified it for us, but it was back behind a stone and wrought-iron gate.

I was relieved to see the owner open the gate and insist that he park our van. We thankfully agreed and met his wife, Martine, who showed us up the stairs to our room. Quickly going to the window, we looked out on a beautiful countryside with a farmhouse below that we later learned had been a stop for the Knights Templar. Since we had recently read Dan Brown's, *Da Vinci Code*, we knew about the Knights.

Dinner that first night was included in our reservation and we were eager to join Martine and Jerome. What an introduction to our foray into French cooking!

Oyster eggs and caviar
Pork roast oozing with smells of rosemary
Wine (of course)
Pasta compote
White asparagus soup
Sautéed garden veggies, eggplant, onions, tomatoes
Fresh garden salad with snow peas
Homemade rolls
More wine
Apple tarte tatin
Tea and coffee... and wine

After wonderful conversation, we pulled ourselves up the stairs to bed! With all the wine, we were asleep in no time!

The next four days were spent exploring the Abbey at Sénanque, the strange stone huts along the roadways, the Sedona-like ochre hills of Roussillon, the glorious poppy fields, the city of Bonnieux (which inspired Peter Mayle's books about Provence), Arles (sites of Van Gogh's paintings), St. Rémy, and Little Venice.

Carolyn debated buying a lovely pottery dish, which I assured her would fit in her carry-on tote, while I couldn't leave a Provence tablecloth in the shop.

We drove to Mont Ventoux and marveled at how the riders in the Tour de France made it up that mountain. There were sausages, cookies and lots of drinks at the top for us, as well as for the bikers.

Coming back to Velázquez on that last day, I winced as I heard the sound of metal meeting stone as I backed a little too close to the wall attempting to get around that troublesome fountain in the center of town. Jerome looked concerned as we pulled up in front of the house for him to park our big van for the last time.

On day five we hugged our hosts and left the House of Blue Shutters for Avignon. We had time to tour the Palace of the Popes before turning in our van. We felt better as the attendant didn't seem to think the dented fender and smashed rear light was a big deal.

Our cooking teacher, Lydie Marshall, sent her husband, Wayne, to meet us at the Auto Europe office and was relieved to see us with only a carry-on-size bag each. I told him that I had been relieved to have my bag! We drove past wineries in the green tree-filled countryside.

Nyons was a charming village, and the Marshall's chateau where our cooking lessons would begin the next day, was in the middle of town. There was a lovely deck outside our room where we could see the bell tower, a statue of the Virgin Mary lit up at night on a nearby hill, and a huge expanse of countryside below. We were high enough to look down on many red rooftops.

Our room was at the top of a stairway, through the billiard room, where there were two stone lions guarding a fireplace. It was easy to get lost finding our room that first day. After freshening up, we went downstairs and began meeting our fellow classmates. The last couple arrived from their week-long hike through the countryside, where they had stopped at bed and breakfasts along the way. I was startled to discover that they lived in Phoenix, Arizona! She had always wanted to go to a French cooking school, and he had always wanted to hike for a week in the countryside, so this vacation satisfied both dreams.

The next morning we found that this was not to be the typical 'classroom' school experience. Our cooking creations were served as dinners in the garden, breakfasts in the lovely dining room with fresh croissants from the town's bakery, homemade jams, lunches as picnics in beautiful neighboring spots beside rivers or quaint bridges; all tastes of French life.

We cooked *Tarte Nyonsaise*, real French fried potatoes, eggplant *a la Neapolitaine* (with Japanese eggplants), asparagus *maltaise*, *galette des rois aux pommes*, *pâte feuilletée*, hand-rolled spaghetti noodles, *bouillabaisse*, potato bread, special strawberry pie, meringue *roulade* with whipped cream, hazelnuts and chocolate, apricot soufflé, and more.

Always with a glass of *Kir*, a popular French cocktail, while we cooked!

One morning at the breakfast table, while Lydie's American engineer husband read *The Wall Street Journal*, she related a story of when they lived in New York City. She taught cooking classes and had been written up in the newspaper. Shortly after the article appeared, she received a call asking if she would give a private lesson for the caller's boss, Mr. Allen. Lydie replied that she was not giving private lessons and hung up. Days later, the woman called again and begged her to reconsider for a very shy Mr. WOODY Allen. Since he was one of her favorites, she gave in and ended up having a wonderful time with Woody Allen in her kitchen.

Sadly, the five days came to an end and Wayne cooked us a farewell brunch of cherries, fresh bread, cheese omelets — and local wine, of course — before driving us back to Avignon to catch the train for the south of France and the Nice airport.

I returned home to Arizona with a notebook of recipes, a few small pieces of pottery, some olives, and my Provence tablecloth. But most importantly, new friends, a shared time with Carolyn, and a grand experience of living in a French chateau. It was also an opportunity to shine my light in France as an American, for I believe we affect the energy of the world wherever we are.

We planned to get together with the couple from Phoenix when we returned to Arizona to host an elegant meal for our married sons. The fall leaves dropped, but no word from them until a Christmas card shared the sad news of her untimely passing. I was grateful that this young sixty-year-old couple had acted on their dreams that summer.

Years later, as I re-live and write of my adventures, I am so grateful for the spiritual connections with others. My opportunities and my choices to say 'yes' to these transformative experiences seem like a personal miracle.

Like my choices of going to Oberlin College, of traveling as a college student, of a similar experience to this one in a cooking school in Italy, these choices and others in the stories that are in this book... these are the every day miracles that expand my life, and awaken my consciousness to the Divine.

Pick-Pocketed in Prague

On a family trip to Prague, we walked to the local tram station to go downtown to the Charles Bridge area (connects one part of the city to another). Standing in a crowd ready to board the tram, my husband suddenly shouted, "Get out of my pocket!"

Two men ran away. Reaching in his pants for his wallet, he realized he had been pick-pocketed. I ran into the tram station to get help but there was no one inside. The tram, and the rest of our family, continued on to its destination. John and I returned to our hotel, told our story to the desk clerk who gave us a form, taken from a large pile of similar forms, to fill out. The attitude of the staff indicated that this was a common occurrence.

In our room, my husband's words blistered my ears. Not liking the negative energy, I put on my bathing suit and headed for the swimming pool where I could escape. I was worried that the birthday dinner, planned by our daughter for her dad that evening, might be ruined by his angry mood.

Swimming laps, I worked on releasing my negative energy. I returned to our room refreshed, and cautiously opened the door. My husband was smiling and joyous. Stunned, I looked for a glass of wine, perhaps, but nothing like that was present.

"I just had the most marvelous experience," he said. "I was sitting here in the chair and I heard a voice say, 'Love them! Love them!'

So, I've been sending the pick-pocketers love and forgiveness. I really heard a voice speak to me!"

We had been reading Dr. David Hawkins's book, *Power vs Force*, that indicates love as the most powerful force in the world. Dr. Hawkins emphasizes that it is not only being a loving person, but visualizing love as a transforming force. That day my husband moved up a level of consciousness in using the energy of love. And now when I hear that someone is hurting I send love, and usually get feedback that the person felt a surge of loving energy.

I have also come to realize that while we cannot prevent negative things from happening in our lives, we can control our feelings and make our own choice as to how we let the occurrence affect our lives. The story we tell and our perception determine our reality. We are more powerful than we realize.

We had a marvelous birthday dinner in Prague that night. But the real miracle was the change in John. Since that night, instead of reacting with anger when negative things happen or when things are said to him, he can now choose to be loving. I always knew he had a big heart, and I will always be grateful for the pick-pocketers in Prague.

The miracle of gratitude is that it shifts
your perception to such an extent
that it changes the world you see.

Robert Holden
British psychologist and author
in the field of positive psychology and well-being

Magical Night in Athens

Our family had just returned from a five-day sailing trip off the coast of Greece, a visit to the island of Chios and then two days on Santorini. This was our last night in Greece and we were tired after our flight from Santorini. We were to leave the hotel for the airport at 7:00 AM the next morning, so everyone agreed to meet in the lobby at 8:30 PM for a simple pizza dinner before retiring for the night.

Daughter Mary had written to a cousin who lived in Athens, telling her of our travel plans and dates. But we had not heard from her and assumed this trip we would not see her.

"Kaites's?" said the hotel clerk as we arrived at the desk to claim our room keys. "We received a call saying that your pickup would be at nine o'clock."

Puzzled about the change in time from seven to nine, we were grateful for the extra two hours in the morning and went to our rooms to freshen up.

My husband and I were the first to arrive in the lobby to wait for the others to go on the pizza run. To our amazement, there was our Greek cousin! She approached, smiling, and wondered if the group was ready to leave for the restaurant. We were startled and indicated that we weren't sure what she was talking about.

"Apparently you didn't receive my reply to Mary's letter telling of our desire to have dinner with you this last night in Athens. My husband is waiting at the restaurant for all of you as our guests."

We picked up the lobby phone and called our four family members to come quickly to meet us.

"We can walk to the restaurant," our cousin stated. The hotel was near the Acropolis, and we peeked between houses to catch a glimpse as we walked the streets.

Music became louder and louder as we approached a *maitre'd* dressed in his finest tux. "Follow me," he advised, and led us to the third level rooftop of this very fancy restaurant.

"*Tikaneiss!*" shouted a man, introducing himself as our cousin's husband. "I've been waiting for you!" I slowly sat down as a new waiter, also attired in a tux, pulled my chair out and directed my sight to the Acropolis. I had a perfect view of it with no obstruction.

We soon were plied with the finest wines, *spanakopita* (a folded pita filled with spinach), *tiropita* (goat cheese), grape leaves with *avgolemono* sauce, olives of various sizes and shapes and other wonderful pita creations. Next came grilled lamb, small roasted potatoes, creamed spinach and, of course, a wonderful Greek salad. We managed to eat the *baklava* and other assorted Greek pastries, coffee or tea and *ouzo* (Greek liquor).

Conversation about the family soon changed to politics, and our host was impressed that our son was a state senator. They talked on and on, but I couldn't take my eyes off the lit Parthenon with the lights from below magically moving from greens to reds to golds as they swept over this ancient ruin dominating the hillside. The moon overhead completed the setting for a magical evening.

After lots of kisses on both cheeks and invitations to visit either in Athens or the States, we started walking home to our hotel. Back at the hotel, close to midnight, I checked with the clerk as to the time for our morning pickup.

"Why, the scheduled time of 7:00 AM," he announced. Apparently the earlier clerk had misunderstood our cousin's message. Her letter was never received before we left for Greece, but the gods were smiling as we managed to have our magical dinner, after all. I'd say the alignment of a loving family connection produced a wonderful evening in Athens.

The Luck of the Chinese Girl

Wonder why others have luck and you don't? Age and wisdom and other's experiences have convinced me that we are creators of our own 'luck.' When we are in alignment or, in simple language, when what we want is congruent with who we are, good things happen. Who we are is a living expression of the Divine. We choose whether to allow Divine light to shine through us and become an expression of the Divine in our NOW. When we are open to our 'intuition' or 'Spirit guides,' we are co-creating our lives.

I remember on a trip up the Yangtze River, meeting a Chinese girl who told me a story that illustrates this principle. Aggy was born in 1974, before the Cultural Revolution when Chinese families were limited to one child. This river guide, on our three-day voyage down the Yangtze River, would not have existed if she had been born in another time.

"My husband and I do not want to have a child," she told me as we sipped a cup of tea. "The competition for good jobs is so intense, if I were to become pregnant I would lose my job. In addition, to raise a child and give it a good life is so expensive now.

"I am so lucky," she continued. "To find true love in China is hard, and I have a wonderful husband. Many girls like to marry foreigners so they can travel outside China. My husband is very handsome, and he is the only son of doctors, so he is rich.

"I am so lucky, as he could have found many girls to marry. My uncle lives in the countryside in a little shack with no electricity and not enough rice, and my mother always told us three children to send money to him. I sent half of my first month's pay to my uncle. I still help him or his family would not eat. There are three children, two girls and one boy. The girls have to help earn money so their brother can go to school. I send money so the girls can go to school.

"I am so lucky that my daddy tried hard to educate all three of us children, even though his parents had been peasants. Daddy was in the army during the Cultural Revolution. His father had died in prison and my grandmother was killed. Chairman Mao was a peasant like my father. His successor, Li, came from privilege and was educated. But the new government told Daddy that he had to retire because he was fifty-five years old. He had to educate children with no income.

"I was so lucky to get into school to be a river guide. There were seventy-three people who applied for this good job. I met my husband, who was studying in Chongqing. We live with my parents to save money. My husband allows me to continue sending money to my cousins for their education. He is a good man.

"I am so lucky to have a kind, understanding and supportive husband. This river job has helped me with my English. I want to go back to school and major in international business. Then we can get our own apartment in Chongqing. My husband's family is rich, but I love the fact that he doesn't ask them for money.

"I am so lucky that my father wanted to help me advance. I have been a river guide for four years. My parents never spent money on themselves. They have not seen the three gorges. Chinese people who have been on this trip are either rich or have connections. It costs $500 for them.

"I am so lucky that my brother and sister also give money to my parents. My brother works for a paper company and has no children. My sister has one child and her husband is in the army."

As our river guide paused to point out the Goddess Peak, she noted that it is rarely seen because of the mist of Wu Gorge. Her luck seemed to be contagious... we were so lucky!

As I said earlier, I don't believe in luck. Aggy's 'luck' seems to be a result of her parent's value of education and their choices to help their children achieve a better life.

What many Americans do not understand is that outside the big cities of China, most Chinese do not have choices, and really do believe in fate and live their lives accordingly.

Aggy saw a bigger life for herself — a bigger pan. She listened to her inner voice and made choices that transformed her life.

If we could see the miracle of a single flower clearly, our whole world would change.

Buddha
Ascetic and sage, on whose teachings Buddhism was founded

Delay into Hooray!!

It was January 21 when John and I awoke to see eight inches of heavy snow bending the tree branches outside our house nearly double as we heard icy pellets knocking on our windows. We jumped out of bed, as we were to depart from the Phoenix airport, one-hundred miles away, that early afternoon for Chile and a cruise to South America.

Cups of tea and worries about our friends, who were also to leave from Prescott in their BMW which had no winter tires, kept us concerned as we scurried to depart. Luggage and our dog loaded in my four-wheel-drive Audi, we slid down our steep hill and found a road with tire tracks out of our hilly neighborhood.

We phoned our friends with the encouraging words that we had made it out to the main road, past downed trees, closed roads and into fog. They shoveled a path down their steep driveway enabling them to pull their luggage to the parked car at the foot of their hill.

We all arrived at our son's house in Phoenix for a quick lunch, transfer of luggage to their van, kiss the dog good-bye, and off we went in the pouring rain to the airport.

First we heard that our plane was circling the airport, not allowed to land due to high winds. Then the announcement informed us that the plane was sent to Texas to refuel.

As the estimated time of departure got later and later, we discovered one other couple on the same trip. The six of us called the cruise ship to announce our predicament, and soon we were in line to re-book our journey to Chile, as the Phoenix Sky Harbor Airport had been closed. Imagine, sunny Arizona's airport closed due to bad weather.

After a night at our son's home, a 3:00 AM phone call from the airport telling us not to hurry as the airport was backed up and our plane to Miami was delayed, we ate breakfast and left for the airport, once again.

"Not to worry," the American Airlines clerk said, we could still make our connection in Miami to Santiago, Chile. Then our challenge was to catch up with the ship, which had left on time. The first port was Puerto Montt, Chile, and there was one flight a day there from Santiago. Yes, we agreed, please book the six of us on that flight!

All went well and we arrived in Miami, then Santiago and then Puerto Montt the following day at 3:30 PM. The nice Chilean driver from the cruise ship arranged to transport us from the airport to a hotel, then offered to drive us out to see the volcanoes and waterfalls special to the area. Since the one couple had arranged to take that trip with the ship the next day, they declined. Our Prescott friends were desperate for a shower and rest while John and I, looking at the blue skies and willing driver, showered and changed in twenty minutes and were on our way.

Gonzalo gave us a first-class tour. The sights were beautiful and he offered to take us to his favorite restaurant in the resort city of Puerto Vargas on our way back to the hotel. Never had such a good fish dinner and glass of wine! It might have been our joy at arriving in Chile and beginning our trip, but maybe not. That fish with a margarita sauce of shrimp and clams was outstanding. John fell asleep in the car on the way back to the hotel, where we met up with our friends who were leaving a so-so dinner at the hotel, and we all were in our beds by 9:00 PM.

The next morning was foggy and cold, the ship arrived as unhappy cruisers left the tender to start their first port tour. The concierge met us and whispered that maybe we hadn't had the worst of the past two days after all. Seems the ocean waters were extremely rough between Santiago and Puerto Montt, the dining rooms had been closed, and most of the passengers were seasick.

Smiling and ready for a relaxed day on the nearly empty ship, John and I waved at the passengers leaving for their bus tour and thanked Divine Order for turning our challenging days into blessings.

Anyone else call a missed departure of a cruise ship a miracle?? When we *allow* what life presents us with and choose to find joy in our circumstances, life seems to present us with miraculous results.

Chapter 7:
Animal Wisdom

She Chose Us
A Bird's Love
Rescue Dog
Honey's Choice
Elephants and Love

She Chose Us

We wanted to have a puppy in our lives, so my husband and I responded to a newspaper ad for new Shih Tzu pups. We were both older and thought a small dog would be best. When the children were home we had Golden Retrievers, but we fancied a little one to jump up in our laps, cuddle with us on the couch, and be able to be controlled on a walk. I had learned in my years of dog ownership that girl doggies tend to stay around home more and not need to mark their territory. So, when I phoned the owner of the litter, I made sure that she had some girls.

I was partial to brown dogs so expressed more interest in her brown and white female pup than the black and white one. We got into the car and rode down the hill to the address. My goodness, the house was ill-kept with lots of discarded stuff in the yard. We almost left, but my husband said that we had scheduled the visit, so we should look at the dog and then leave.

The woman came out in an old housedress and carried a tiny brown and white bundle. She advised us that we could not come closer to the house as it was her mother's and she had a pit bull inside who was not friendly. We were almost glad that the puppy had lazy eyes and no energy and was not appealing at all, so we wouldn't be tempted to take her. I thanked the tired looking woman and said we would be on our way. She explained that she had come from Alabama to care for her mother. The dog was pregnant and the puppies had been born here in Prescott. It was a difficult birth and the veterinarian charged an arm and a leg. We were sorry to hear her story, but we turned to leave.

"Let me get the other female pup... might as well look at her since you're here." I guess we were too polite to say no, but we edged toward the car out front. Down the front steps she came, this time holding an alert little black and white soul.

This pup sure did not look like a Shih Tzu, with the typical pushed-in face but my, was she cute, and so lively and personable. Her coloring was lovely, balanced on both sides of her head and with the cutest tail. Then she looked at me and there was no doubt that her eyes said, "I belong to you."

The owner held firm to her advertized price, acceptable for a pedigreed dog, which we were sure this one wasn't, but a little much for a fifty-seven variety. "Oh no, she is an Imperial Shih Tzu. I have papers, but I left them in Alabama in my hurry to come help mother... $300, please."

My husband looked helplessly at me and asked if I really thought this was our dog. As I looked into her imploring eyes, I replied, "She thinks she is." And, that was the beginning of our love affair with Katie.

The first night we had prior plans, so left her in her crate with our neighbor to babysit. He let her out to play for a few minutes and called her Little Shit from then on. I think you can guess why.

There was no doubt who ran our household and who was definitely an alpha dog. Sometimes the Universe gives you what you need rather than what you want or think you need. I learned to express myself more strongly after she came.

We hired a trainer to come to the house and help us get the upper hand, but since he arrived with doggie treats in his pocket, he trained her to jump up on every visitor, convinced that they had come just to see her and would have a cookie in their pocket, for sure. As much as we spoke, "Heel," she would always lead the way on our walks.

Since both my husband and I have strong egos, it has helped us to know that getting along is more important than getting your way.

Katie jumped up on our bed as soon as morning broke and put her face into my husband's saying, "It's time for our walk." She enabled both of us to stay in physical shape by walking around the neighborhood and up and down our steep driveway.

She loved our grandkids when they came to visit and jumped up and down when our neighbor came, often with a treat. As our faith journey came to bring us the wisdom that we are all one, Katie expanded that to include those in the animal kingdom. We know she communicated with us and our hearts were connected.

When the black bags came down from the shelf in the closet, she would start to mourn our absence. But, when she arrived at the vet's for boarding, Katie wagged her tail and the techs told us how good she was and how much they loved her. It took us miles into our journey before the heavy lump in our chests eased and we could look forward to our trip and not backward to already missing Katie.

- 133 -

Katie at play.

My 75th birthday year, the plan was to rent a restored farm house in Tuscany, Italy, and invite the children and grandchildren. It was almost a year of planning and excitement as we looked forward to this special time. We had a friend who was a dog sitter and especially in tune with energy and holistic medicine. She came over to meet Katie and we knew we had provided the very best friend for the two weeks we would be across the pond.

A month before the trip, Katie manifested a large swelling on her hind leg. After a vet's visit and blood evaluations, we gave Katie an antibiotic and in a week the swelling was reduced and her energy returned. Two weeks later, she stopped eating and the vet found a tumor in her abdomen. He shook his head and said that we could take her to Phoenix to an oncologist and give her steroids, but this was only to delay the inevitable.

We took her home to love. We knew she would let us know when it was time. I cooked special chicken and calves liver. We rejoiced when she'd eat, go outside to walk the driveway with us or ask to go for a ride in the car. After conferring with our friend, we signed a paper giving permission to put Katie down, if necessary, while we were in Italy.

Again, we were pulled with not wanting to leave her on the one hand, and the anticipation of being with family in Tuscany on the other. I looked into her eyes, and behind the pain was such a look of love and connection that I knew we could never be truly separated. It was not quite time for her to be put down before we left.

We said our goodbye's wondering if we would see her when we returned. The day came when we phoned home from Italy and were told that Katie's time had come. We believe she chose it. We were comforted in our grief to learn that Katie's favorite tech had her arms around her as the vet eased her pain. Katie has been in both of our dreams and we sensed her spirit filling us with gratitude for the years we had with her in our lives.

After returning from Tuscany, we had a new project. We had loved a table off the patio at the farm house in Italy where we could sit and talk, read, eat, or play games. The house cat would come and purr under the table. Now that we no longer needed a fence to keep Katie from roaming, there was a perfect place off the patio ~ where Katie used to sit and talk to the neighbor dog, Cooper ~ for a table with vines going up the posts and over the top. It would be just like at the farm house.

There are trees overhead, a water feature with its sounds of connection to all, and we have a sign on the side of the house letting you know that this wonderful spot is 'Katie's Korner.'

A Bird's Love

Bam! A bird had flown into the sliding glass door separating our bedroom from the outside deck, and was lying still. Suddenly, a feathered friend landed on the deck, pecked on the hurt back and quietly sat next to her buddy.

I sent love to the injured bird and ran for my camera. When I returned, I saw the bird's partner with his beak on her back, and they stood like that for almost five minutes. The photograph above is what I took that day, just before the two birds hopped off the deck onto the ground and then flew away.

In the animal world, there are times we can see evidence of and learn of compassion.

> Once you study natural science and the miracles of creation, if you don't turn into a mystic you are not a natural scientist.
>
> Albert Hofmann
> Swiss scientist

Rescue Dog

It had been over a year since we lost our dear Katie dog. My husband missed company on his morning walk, I missed her presence and affection in the house, and our grandchildren just missed her. We had tried to adopt a Labrador Retriever that a friend of our daughter-in-law suggested was a good match for us. But we were embarrassed to have to return Kira because she was too big for us to handle and besides, she jumped our low backyard fence at will!

Friday our local paper, *The Daily Courier,* had a photo of a little black and white doggie that looked a lot like our Katie. Since there were so many interested in this little angel, there was to be an auction Saturday afternoon. My husband looked longingly at the photo, aware that he would be on a meditation retreat Saturday and Sunday. I had planned to spend Friday night in Phoenix with a friend and go to the Desert Botanical Garden early Saturday morning to take photos.

Leaving Phoenix later that morning to drive up the Rim towards Prescott, I kept seeing that photo of the little black and white dog. I consciously don't know why I found myself parking outside the Humane Society in plenty of time before the auction.

Being a believer that guidance comes from within, as well as a practitioner of muscle testing, I asked myself, "Is the black and white dog the one for us?"

Surprised by the 'No' response my muscle testing gave me, I asked, "Is the right and best dog for us here today?"

Surprise again. 'Yes.'

"Can I help you?" the kind woman at the Humane Society desk asked. Not ready to give up on what seemed like our perfect dog, I asked to see the little black and white dog going up for auction that day. She pointed the way to the cage and off I went, ready to believe that my muscle testing had gone awry.

Barking led me to the correct cage where the little black and white dog was humping the male dog in the cage constantly. The dog also seemed really nasty!

I apologized to my muscle testing, gave a quick grateful inner blessing and moved down the row of cages looking for 'our right dog' but none resonated with me.

Since my husband was away, and I didn't have another commitment, I sat outside to ponder the dog situation. I asked a staff member walking a large dog if I could join her for the walk. She was friendly and interested in what had brought me there that morning.

After hearing my sad tale, she motioned for me to follow her over to Receiving. We went down that row of cages of newly acquired animals and she stopped in front of a cage with a cute little Cocker Spaniel looking up at us with longing eyes.

"She has been here a week. We're waiting if the person who 'chipped' her returns our call. This is the last day, and later we will take her over to the adoption side of the building."

I kept looking at this critter that didn't bark, was wagging her tail and seemed to be saying, "I am YOUR dog!"

The attendant asked if I would like to spend a few minutes with her outside in the yard. I eagerly nodded yes, and out we went.

My new-found friend was affectionate, peed in the grass, and seemed utterly delighted to be free and outside. I asked the dog's age and was told six or seven years. That seemed good; old enough to be trained and yet enough years left to be a pal to two older folks.

"Are you over sixty-five?" the attendant asked.

"Oh yes," I replied.

"Well then, there is no charge, you get a free vet's exam, five pounds of food, and you can bring her back if she doesn't bond with your husband." Sounded win-win to me!

John arrived home the next morning, saw Katie's bed back in our bedroom and with sparkling eyes started looking for the black and white dog that I must have bid on and won at the auction. Around the corner came this sweet little honey-colored Cocker Spaniel going right up to him to be petted. Surprised, he heard my tale of rescue and put the leash on her for a walk.

Now, three happy years later with Honey, I am more than ever a believer in intuition, muscle testing, and allowing the Universe to guide us to a miracle.

Honey's Choice

Honey was now ten years old. This day she curled up and wouldn't move, eat, look at us, or make a sound. It almost hurt as badly as when one of the kids was sick.

We took her to our vet who said she had pancreatitis, gave her a shot and sent her home with us hoping for the best.

That night, I awoke to find John lying on the floor with his arm on Honey and speaking softly to her.

"We love you very much and want you to get well. But, if you need to go, know that we love you and want what's best for you. It's your choice."

I tip-toed back to bed, and he returned shortly after.

In the morning we were greeted with Miss Honey up on her four legs and wagging her tail. She had made her choice. A miracle... answered prayer... but her choice! It was not time to part and we could love each other awhile longer.

Elephants and Love

On safari in Africa, my experiences there led me to realize how special elephants are in their caring and compassion. Later, when I returned home, a friend shared this story.

Lawrence Anthony, who had grown up in the bush and was known as the 'Elephant Whisperer,' saved two violent rogue elephant herds destined to be shot as pests because of the destruction they had caused in South Africa.

He brought them over six-hundred miles to his game reserve to be rehabilitated. Later he wrote a book of this experience, *The Elephant Whisperer: My Life with the Herd in the African Wild.*

In his book Anthony gives a detailed account of how he tried to build trust with these amazing creatures by talking to Nana, the matriarch of the first herd, explaining they would all be killed if they broke out of the reserve. But they found a way to escape.

Then it occurred to him that he had to live with them to save their lives. He would live with the herd, feed them, talk to them, and be with them day and night. And it worked.

Anthony eventually retired and moved away. But when he died in March 2012, the first of those two wild elephant herds that he had saved years before arrived at his home the following Sunday, and the second herd, a day later. They had walked about twelve hours to come and mourn the death of one of their own.

This photograph was taken from Anthony's book, *The Elephant Whisperer.* Anthony wrote other books about his conservation experiences to raise international awareness of the animal crises in South Africa and to raise money for conservation in his reserve in Zululand and his environmental group, The Earth Organization.

They all hung around for about two days before making their way back into the bush.

Amazing! Love is a powerful force – some say that what we call God, is the vibration or energy of love.

I was privileged to interact with an elephant family one morning while on our African safari and I loved their gentle energy.

Our guide for that trip was Lynne Leakey. She had married into the Leakey family of Kenya who had researched man's origins, as well as protected elephants.

We so enjoyed the morning with these elephants that Lynne had set up for us to meet.

I have been privileged to witness the deep love that animals have been able to add to our lives and our world and that morning took this photograph.

Chapter 8:
My 'Tuesday' Group

Miracles in My 'Tuesday' Group
The Gifts of Sight
A Moment for the Leader
Happily Ever After
Spiritual Sight
Sending Love
Mandy's Miracle Story
The Newcomer
Jean's Belief
An Angel Unaware
P.S.

Miracles in My 'Tuesday' Group

Members of the group started experiencing physical challenges. One person had a detached retina, another a heart attack, a third a broken leg, and then another developed PMR (*polymyalgic rheumatica*).

We had been studying Abraham's DVDs, bringing the principles alive in our lives. Some had even attended workshops. What were these challenges about?

Well, we've gotten a bigger pan of understanding. We now believe that challenges can be blessings as they cause us to examine our lives and see through expanded eyes.

Too often we judge things as good or bad, right or wrong. But there are usually many ways to see something, solve a problem or worship God.

Oprah Winfrey says that, "No experience is wasted... Everything in life is happening to grow you up, to fill you up, to help you become more of who you were created to be."

We often look back and see how what was once considered a negative was the very thing that stimulated growth in our lives.

If you need a miracle, call me.
I'm a Specialist.
God

The Gifts of Sight

At the beginning of each gathering of our growth group, we share miracles that happen in our lives. We have become aware lately that each one of us has had a physical challenge this past year. We ask why?

Formerly we thought that if we were in alignment with Spirit, life would be without serious problems. We now see that these challenges are opportunities for each of us to go deeper into ourselves. These guide us to our very essence.

One week our loving hostess, Alice, told of going to her optometrist for a regular checkup and was advised to see a specialist. Her retina was in danger of being more fully detached. She has had difficulty seeing with her left eye for years.

After two hours of surgery, the doctor was unable to attach the retina, and she was in pain from this lengthy attempt. Week after week we were aware of her constant blinking and that she was having increasing difficulty keeping her good eye open.

I suggested that she go to my optometrist for a second opinion. He had been a rocket scientist before going into optometry school and was smart as well as committed to solving problems.

Surprisingly to me, his opinion was that it would be impossible to re-attach her retina. I was disappointed. However, he told her to stop blinking! She has, and now her eye waters less and her vision is more comfortable. The doctor was grateful for her letter expressing gratitude for this small miracle.

Just the other day Alice asked me how this book was coming along, and commented, "I hope you are including some of your wonderful photographs."

I wondered if I should since my best photographs do not directly illustrate many of the stories. Last night I couldn't sleep and was drawn to read the book, *The Untethered Soul*, by Michael Singer. This book enhanced my understanding of who I really am. I am one who sees.

Photography has changed the way I look at life. It has widened and expanded and deepened what I focus on, what I care about, what I pay attention to... I appreciate that your eyes can open your heart wider. A love of photography has given me something in common with my granddaughters.

Could I share what I see through photography? Is this realization a miracle coming out of my alignment? Would some photos taken on my journeys answer my life-long question as to why I love to travel or why my adult children ask me to take photos of their families? Or could it simply be that because I love to take photos, that at my essence there is joy in my life that also brings pleasure to others?

That is what Abraham, through Esther Hicks, says is the purpose of life. They did not say that we have to be the best at what we do, rather that we *seek joy*.

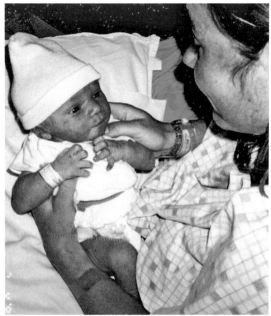

As I was writing this paragraph, I saw a televised feature about a woman who takes photographs of newborns who are not expected to survive. She calls her service, "Now I Lay Me Down to Sleep."

One of my friends had shared that she wonders what her baby boy, who died shortly after birth, looked like since time has erased his little face from her memory.

What a beautiful purpose for photography.

A miracle happened: another day of life.

Paulo Coelho
Brazilian lyricist and novelist

A Moment for the Leader

He usually asks us to share. This day he was hunched over a thick book he said he had been studying since we last met. Slowly he looked up at us and asked, "What does eternity mean to you?"

After a few answers like, 'infinite' and 'no ending,' he said, "Then why haven't I received my miracle?"

Abraham has answered that very same question to someone on the 'hot seat' at a conference with, "there must be resistance within you."

One of us asked, "What miracle are you asking for?"

We were in for a serious session. This man was raised by parents who rarely complimented him or said anything positive to him at all. Now he wondered if he was great, good enough... or even helpful.

This from a retired psychiatrist, a doctor trained to take care of everybody but himself. A man who devoted hours of his time each week with two or three groups of seekers and had successfully raised seven children, plus a a grandson who recently graduated from college.

He was currently studying *A Course in Miracles* and we were slowly experiencing his growing belief in his worth, and his right to be joyful. He was close to even believing in his own Divinity, not just ours. He had seen the change in us. How many times has he confronted me and others with, "Do you believe you are a part of God?"

"I want to believe I have eternal life... that I am Divine, that I am a part of God," he continued. "Intellectually, I know it. But I want to FEEL it!"

That word *God* has so many meanings to so many people that we usually use Creator, Spirit, Universal Intelligence, etc. However, we in the group all believe there is a Creative energy that is in all things in this world and we all have a spark of that within. When in alignment, we vibrate with more power.

Satisfied that this was the most he was going to get from us, we moved on. As much as we love him, we cannot <u>do it</u> for him. To transform our minds, means belief... "As ye believe, so shall it be done unto you." (Matthew: 8:13)

Uncovering our own resistance takes deep probing, allowing feedback and guidance from within, meditation, and focus. We all seek to have more clarity, even our dear leader.

The most incredible thing about miracles,
is that they happen.

G.K Chesterton

Happily Ever After

Yesterday John wanted me to write a story about him and his miracle. But, the story didn't end 'Happily Ever After' like he wanted so, no miracle.

Isn't that like LIFE? We pray, expect Spirit to answer our prayers the way we want, and how often does that work? Loved ones pass on, some are healed and others aren't. We receive the new house or car we bid on and sometimes we don't. I could go on and on.

You may remember when the papers were full of the two prisoners in upper state New York who cut their way out of their prison cell and escaped into the Adirondack woods. On the eleventh day of their freedom, my husband had used kinesiology by muscle testing to try to locate them. He learned from Dr. David Hawkins and Dr. Bradley Nelson.

He has great confidence in its value for those few who use and believe in it. I feel that it works up to a point, and in individual ways. For me, other energy methods are more effective than muscle testing as I sense that I can influence my hands. John however, has experienced good results by circling his thumbs and forefingers.

He first used it in an attempt to locate the sunken Malaysian airplane that probably went down in the ocean near Australia. For days the search centered near Malaysia, but John muscle-tested and believed the plane was located south of that area. He bought maps and through muscle testing located the coordinates. Since Fox News TV asked for viewer input, he emailed and phoned. No reply.

Praying to receive guidance about further direction, since he believed that God wanted those bodies recovered and closure for the families, we pursued. I even had a dream to research salvage companies, did so and called one who had recovered a ship off the coast of Italy and who had an office in Australia. Thanks, but no further interest in our information.

Unfortunately, 'traditional' methods of research are more acceptable and not enough 'scientific' research has been done on kinesiology to give it the necessary credibility.

Back to the escapees. John again bought maps and circled the location based upon the coordinates he received with his muscle testing. He then phoned the New York State Police's tips line and was told that his information wasn't concrete enough for them to act on. Bummer.

"Why would Spirit give me this gift and this information, in the middle of the night, to boot, if I wasn't to act on it?" he agonized.

Sunday we had a guest speaker at church and she suggested that often our guidance, such as John received, is for our own challenge to grow. John pondered this thought, and asked for my opinion. I thought it made sense. John is a retired successful businessman and now likes recognition for his spiritual growth.

Could this be John's blessing in the inspiration to locate the prisoners? He uses kinesiology with each decision he is faced with, with good results. Could this be enough? Right now he doesn't think so and says it would be a great story to add to my book if somehow his location would prove to lead to the prisoners or the Malaysian airplane. That would be dramatic!

It is my belief, however, that the best ending would be one in which each of you would believe that Spirit has gifted you with just the right blessings within for you to be a worthwhile and loved person. That your Light within would shine and your life would be a gift to others, as is my John's.

How often do we wish we were more than we are, or feel that we are not good enough? When the truth is, we are perfect the way we are. How's that for a 'Happily Ever After' ending to this story.

Miracles are reminders
that we do not know everything.

Ervin Welsh
British novelist, playwright and short story writer

Spiritual Sight

As I have aged, my optometrist told me that I have glaucoma and need eye drops to regulate the eye pressure. What was this challenge telling me? I wondered what I was not aware of in my life, or whether I was looking too often superficially and not focusing inwardly enough. I had lots of questions, no answers.

I also am at the age where cataracts often develop. When I was recovering from the new lens insertion, it became obvious there was a problem. When I had the cataract surgery, a complication occurred that necessitated removing one lens for another. All in all, it took quite a bit of doing; I had to see the doctor daily for over a month.

Now using my spiritual sight instead of focusing on my physical sight, what has come to me from this event is that I was quick to offer help to others, to ask Spirit to send love and healing energy to where it was needed. But seeing inwardly for my own healing was more challenging.

Now I realize I like myself better, and that I am worth asking Spirit for healing when needed. Challenges are there for all of us to go within and learn to love ourselves. From out of problems can come growth when we see ourselves with new eyes.

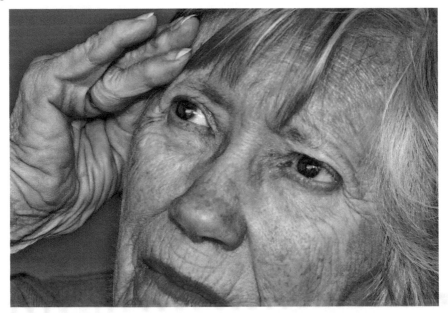

Sending Love

Susie, a group member, exploded with the news that her boss in her new job at a nursery school was constantly criticizing her and she wasn't going to take it anymore. Knowing that she was saving for a travel trailer to move to a lovely piece of land that she owned in a nearby state, we looked askance at this threat to quit her job with children and lose income.

"Have you considered sending your boss love and changing the energy between you?" one of the group asked.

"No, she has been on my case since I started and the other teachers all notice it."

Abraham says that you cannot change other people's behavior, you can only change your own. Believing that she knew in her heart that this was an approach that would help, we sent her love and returned to watching the current DVD, knowing that she would reconsider when the time was right.

Susie could hardly wait for the group to start the following week and she beamed while telling us that this teacher had been so nice to her all week.

"How did that happen?" our group leader asked expectantly.

With a sheepish grin on her face she replied, "Oh, I just sent her love."

She had moved beyond her 'normal' of the blame game with victimhood, to risk broadening her vision... that of being her true self, that of risking expanding her consciousness and *becoming* a new normal.

I thought of the retired Catholic priest, Richard Rohr, who wrote in his book, *Falling Upward*, "If you don't transform your suffering, you will transmit it." Susie showed us that transformation works.

This incident reminded me of Marianne Williamson's words that "faith in miracles turns out to be not the most blind, but rather the most visionary way of perceiving the world."

Everything
is a spark
of that eternal radiance.
Why flee
from the world
in order to find it
when you
yourself
are already on fire?

Adyashanti

Mandy's Miracle Story

Mandy has been in our group of consciousness raisers from the beginning. She has reported lots of miracles, but none moved me as much as the one last week.

Telling about her separation years before from her husband and responsibility for half of his debts, she recalled struggling to do this from the rented place where she was living. When the house next door went on the market, she knew it was the perfect house for her.

Barely out of debt, she wondered how it would be possible. She set an intention, and then talked to others who were in a position to support her dream. Soon enough money accumulated for the down payment and ownership was on its way. Mandy then revealed how she has done similar acts of kindness since; in other words, 'paid it forward.'

I remembered how my husband and I had acted when we heard that our divorced pastor had fallen in love with a single mother of two, and they planned to marry. Each was living in a small apartment. The intention was set for an end unit in a newly built section of homes.

John asked our pastor for the names of ten close friends and then asked each if they could contribute $500 towards a down payment. It is twenty years later and that couple still lives in that home. How quickly do we stop at praying for answers, and forfeit our opportunity to participate in miracles?

I had been talking about the high cost of publishing a book and whether this one was going to be possible with its color photographs. Talk about hearing your own words!

Seems like it's always easier to believe it is possible for others, but not us. Her gift to me was sharing her story. My gift to you was in setting the intention to publish. Focusing my mind allowed the transformation from fears of lack, as well as distractions from the busy conflicts of ordinary life to fade and let timing allow a miracle.

The Newcomer

Loretta was the newest member of our group. She wondered if she belonged as she thought each of us was further along in the growth process. She listened for much of the time at first.

This particular day we were exploring Abraham's concept of *being* versus *doing*, and how we can only change ourselves and be an authentic person, not focus on helping others to be different in life. (We should do what brings us joy and allow others to be responsible for their own lives.)

We often help others get into 'doing,' and believe that it is a good thing to do for THEM. Today the focus was on how that really is a means of avoiding OUR own needs.

During this discussion we noticed that Loretta was struggling to keep from crying, and our leader encouraged her to 'let it out.'

Slowly, with a choked voice, she looked amazed as she realized that this was what she had done her entire life. When she hadn't received the praise she wanted, she blamed others. She had expectations of her husband and was always disappointed with his response to her.

As she realized that her job in life is to be a loving person, she smiled and acknowledged that she could do that. She realized that she could only control her feelings; she could only make choices for herself.

No one could decide what someone else needs or should do.

Our leader smiled as he pointed at her and said, "Now, her new awareness is a miracle!"

We seldom recognize that the insights we each make on our journeys are small miracles making our lives more joyful. Does it last? Usually not!

Loretta teared up the next week as she said that 'Van Gogh' was back. She had called herself Van Gogh because her life was one of suffering. She told us of a dream she had had in which the only way she could get out of suffering was to cut her foot off. Through her sobs she stammered, "There is no way to escape my life of suffering."

A woman in the group leaned forward and suggested that since it was a dream, or a made-up story, why not visualize a clamp around her

foot that she could spring open? That way she was out of the trap and she still had her foot and could get away.

The teary face changed to smiles and Van Gogh had to go back in the shadows. She was reminded that sometimes it takes experiencing the miracle over again until it is strong enough to last.

We're dealing with life-long habits and beliefs here. We shouldn't be discouraged when we don't 'get it' the first time. We recognized that all of us in the group had grown in wisdom and joy and that it sometimes takes several lessons, both present and in Spirit, to achieve our results.

Jean's Belief

"My miracle is that I BELIEVE!"

So spoke this 80-year-old, five-foot-tall woman who was glowing as she shared with our Tuesday group.

Jean had been coping with back pain for months, if not years. She explained that she had *scoliosis*, an abnormal curvature of the spine. This dear one walked slightly bent over and would list to one side. Her usual sunny disposition was resigned lately to her condition and age, and she kind of enjoyed being touched by healers because of her aching back, but not this day.

I had noticed that her bicycle was parked outside on the porch. She had not ridden down the street to our group meeting for awhile, citing her back pain as the reason. But the bike was there this day.

She and I had shared that as we both were now in our eighties, and I had been challenged since a teen-aged basketball player with another 's' word (*spondylothesis*) we had back pain in common (my fourth and fifth vertebrae had slipped to the side of my spine).

However, she exploded with, "My miracle is that I BELIEVE!"

Believe what?

"My change is that I now believe I can be free of pain and I am. I believe that our bodies are made to heal themselves and I choose not to have any more pain. I haven't had any pain for days now and am back riding my bike!"

Our Abraham group had agreed with the theory that our thoughts create our reality. But do we really own that truth? Did Jean or I test it out on our back pain before? Did we Really Believe??

Well she did last week and glows with success. I have noticed my back hurts much less since deciding I didn't need it to hurt anymore.

Did we affect our leader who proposed the miracle question?

Sheepishly, he confessed, "Why, if I believe and trust God, then I'll have to go along with the Universe's will. I'm afraid to trust as I don't want to give up control."

That is his decision. What's yours?

We live on a blue planet
that circles around a ball of fire,
next to a moon that moves the sea...
and you don't believe in miracles?

An Angel Unaware?

Who told him that he 'should' keep his face down as he walked on the sidewalk recently? Tawfia described the stranger who made that comment as he was passing him by, as a normal looking guy. However, it triggered a tape from his deceased parents.

This former Iraqi had been told over and over that it was dangerous for dark skinned folks like 'them' to ever call attention to themselves. Tawfia commented that as a bright student in South America, he had often been cheated of a good grade or placement in an above-average class. This protective behavior continued in his jobs, as he was often passed over for promotions and, of course, he never called attention to himself by challenging a boss's decision. He just moved on.

Tawfia realized that he had been afraid when the stranger told him to keep his head down while walking on that street. He made an appointment to process this with our Tuesday group leader, a retired psychiatrist.

Dr. Len encouraged him to tell us about his encounter at our Tuesday group gathering. Tawfia looked up at us as he said that he

was tired of always feeling afraid of the consequences of speaking up for himself, tired of moving from country to country and city to city to avoid being treated as a second class citizen.

Our group focuses on recognizing our inherent goodness as children of God, created in the image of, and having the qualities of Spirit.

In our our group Tawfia had felt accepted as an equal and was beginning to own his real birthright.

The group believes that when we each are ready to 'get a bigger pan' and move up in consciousness, the

Universe provides us with a challenging opportunity. Could this stranger have been such a person in Tawfia's life? Perhaps even an angel and evidence of a miracle, because he was now challenging his early decision to lower his head. He now raises his head and smiles at all of us.

Miracles are not contrary to nature,
but only contrary to what we know about nature.

Saint Augustine

P.S.

Genna, my editor, and I scheduled Friday as the final day to tie up loose ends on my book in readiness to submit it to the publisher.

Where was I on Friday? Flat on my back in the hospital!

So, I'm adding a postscript to the book. One of the loose ends was the title! I had used *Miracle Moments* as the working title, but questioned whether it would appeal to the readers I most wanted to reach. I worried that it might not cause a non-spiritual reader to consider this collection of short stories that challenged one to expand horizons or 'get a bigger pan' to hold new concepts.

As Einstein said, you either believe nothing is a miracle, or you believe that everything is a miracle. I believe and, through my stories, I advocate that everything is a miracle.

Genna came into my hospital room with a lovely heart-shaped necklace and the advice to not listen to anyone else's comments about the title but to listen to my heart. You see, I was in the hospital recovering from a stroke. Could pressure I put on myself be the cause? I didn't think so, and others didn't see me as a person who doesn't listen to myself. However...

Four days later, when I attended my Tuesday group, Len, our leader, started the session with, "Elizabeth has a miracle."

I truly did, as I had no aftereffects from the TIA (Transient Ischemic Attack) or a full blown stroke. Lots of love came my way.

The very next day Alice, Len's wife, phoned shocking me with the news that Len had had a stroke Tuesday night after our meeting, and was paralyzed on his entire right side.

One of our members, who lives across the street and had seen the ambulance and fire engine arrive, went to the hospital with Alice. Later that night, the two women sent Len divine healing energy and love, and watched in amazement as his right side slowly regained movement.

Wonder why I was guided to name the book, *Miracle Moments*???

Chapter 8:
Reflections

Gifts of Meditation
Making the Sun Stand Still
Evolutionary Enlightenment
Reflections
More Reflections...
Listen and Love: The Core of Powerful Relationships
Expanding Consciousness to Better Serve Spirit
Wrapping Up...

Stop acting so small.
You are the universe in ecstatic motion.

Rumi

Gifts of Meditation

I raised my children in Maryland. An Oberlin classmate lived nearby and one day we all gathered in the woods by her house and learned to meditate using transcendental meditation.

In meditation, a person will experience a depth, a focus, a oneness that is an indicator of 'another level.' Usually these times are unplanned, rather a response to our 'allowing' whatever can happen in the moment. How often do we program stillness into our daily lives and consequently receive guidance?

Stillness or meditation can also be a walk in the woods, prayer, certain music, dreams, or a nap. They are all times when we quiet our minds. It is especially difficult in this age of smart phones and video games to live at the speed of life and not the pace of machines.

Silence is not the absence of anything, but the presence of everything.

Making the Sun Stand Still

I was seeking inspiration for the talk I was to give Wednesday night at church. Working at my laptop, I found a new article by respected Unity writer, Jim Rosemergy, *Making the Sun Stand Still*. In reading it, I thought about times when it seemed that time moved so quickly while other times it seemed to move slowly. But, standing still?

Rosemergy had written of beginning each counseling session with five minutes of silence. Many of us meditate to quiet our minds and listen to the still, small voice inside. During these times, we enter a state of consciousness where Spirit is present, and time seems to stand still.

Rosemergy suggests that perhaps we have entered the realm where there is no time. When we return to our world, the consciousness of the Universe clings to us and we become far more productive and insightful. Silence is a timeless realm, and we can enter it by being still and giving our attention to the Spirit within.

Another way to make the sun stand still is to be in the NOW moment, which Rosemergy calls the threshold of the infinite.

Others speak of the inner place where creative imagination resides. Some refer to moments of bliss, feelings of oneness, or experiencing an epiphany. I believe they are all speaking of the same experience.

A Common Thread includes a story about learning to be in the world. I wrote of being aware of a challenge, reflecting, and then going into action to counter it. When I pause to center, I am in higher consciousness, and the action that follows is more likely to be one of love and, therefore, more effective. When we have loving conversations with those in our ordinary lives, our unique radiant core aligns with theirs, and our environment is enhanced.

> Each morning we are born again.
> What we do today is what matters.
>
> Buddha
> Ascetic and sage, on whose teachings Buddhism was founded

To know yourself as the Being underneath the thinker,
the stillness underneath the mental noise,
the love and joy underneath the pain,
is freedom, salvation, enlightenment.

Eckhart Tolle

Evolutionary Enlightenment

It was exactly 5:00 PM and the interview with Andrew Cohen, the author of the newly published book, *Evolutionary Enlightenment*, was beginning on the internet. In addition to Andrew, guests Ken Wilber and Jean Houston were to be on the program. I was eager to listen as several of my friends and I were going to discuss this book. I so wanted it to be good!

Jean started with the usual compliments and then stated, "Our goal is to live large!"

I was reminded of Barbara Marx Hubbard's focus on the fourteen billion years of life on Earth, the enormous manifestation that we see all around us and the impulse today for so many people, me included, to be more fully who we are.

I agree with Barbara, and now Andrews, that whatever Creator is, that is within me as well.

What excites me most is the thought that as we have gone from *doing* to *being*... now we are challenged to *'becoming.'* I really like that thought. It includes the concept of our oneness with others and all in the Universe.

And these days scientists are telling us that between us and stuff, there is a lot going on! There is energy, inner development that exists in us and in the entire Universe. There are bigger words and loftier concepts to talk about this, but it is enough that I resonate with the truth of it all. It is exciting to me to think that there is greater value in coming together with others who have desire to move in the same trajectory at this time in my life. Seems richer somehow than ending with Being.

Becoming... I like it!!

Reflections

I used to think that Jesus walking on water, turning water into wine or healing beggars defined miracles. Stories in this book reveal miracles in our ordinary lives. Perhaps, even simply walking on earth is a miracle.

Since I believe that each of us is a part of the essence of the Universe and Source (Creator or God), I am convinced that when we are in alignment with our Source, miracles occur naturally. We are challenged to realize that when our souls connect in a beautiful oneness with each other and with Source, we have become co-creators.

Gary R. Renard, in his book, *The Disappearance of the Universe*, says that miracles are habits... 'a miracle is a shift in perception over to Source's way of thinking.' One miracle is no less important than another. The beauty of miracles is that they are happening now if we can change our perception and see them... now. We can benefit from them... now. We can learn from them... now. My earlier thinking left miracles in the past or set the criteria so high, it would take many years and big challenges for them to occur. We don't have to wait for a guru to 'perform' a miracle like I thought.

You might ask, how do we get in alignment with Source? I find that when my emotions are in line with my goals, that works. For example, when I want to intensify love, I think of someone or something that brings up my feelings of love. Sometimes it is a remembrance of a dear thing a grandchild has done, a thoughtful word from a person in my life, the devotion of a dear animal friend, or even a beautiful sunset.

My vibration is stronger and the alignment becomes greater. I have learned to ALLOW stuff to happen as Spirit wills. Now when someone asks for help, I send a vibration of Love and allow Source to control.

What brings joy to you... and are you doing it? Are you afraid of your own Power? I believe that as we realize who we really are, claim the divinity within, become aware of the miracles in our own lives, we affect the environment around us for the better. Others feel our love and positive energy and become more positive themselves.

I challenge you to set an intention to be the Love that others around you need; to listen to your divine inner guidance; to light up with joy at the simple miracles in your life. One of the truest tests of spiritual maturity or higher consciousness is seeing the miraculous in our everyday lives. Know that your life is full of simple miracles. You are better for your knowing and, I believe, the positive energy improves our world.

> If you stumble about believability,
> what are you living for?
> Love is hard to believe, ask any lover.
> Life is hard to believe, ask any scientist.
> God is hard to believe, ask any believer.
> What is your problem with hard to believe?
>
> Yann Martel
> Spanish-born Canadian author of *Life of Pi*

More Reflections...

What if we choose to live our lives as though everything is a miracle? Siddhartha Gautama, the founder of Buddhism, sought to understand the cause of suffering. As he focused his mind, he believed that attachment to the material world was the cause. When people showed compassion for others, their minds were freed from suffering.

Others have written about happiness resulting from loving others. Recently, Morgan Freeman narrated a series of programs entitled, *The Story of God,* on the National Geographic Channel. In one segment he stated that many religions are miracle-based, and when he sought the source of the Higher Power, he found that it was inside each person.

In another segment, Freeman was talking with a lama in India, and the discussion included, "We are inspired by our inner God. When we are, we can do miracles." And the lama continued, "So after all, what is a miracle other than transforming the human mind?"

Your life is not too ordinary for miracles. Much of what we call 'miraculous' starts in the mind. Set your mind to transform any limiting beliefs. There is something that unites us, a common thread within, and we inspire each other. A belief in miracles gives us hope and Morgan Freeman says, "that belief drives us to create reality out of possibility."

So after all, what is a miracle other than transforming the human mind?

Listen and Love:
The Core of Powerful Relationships

When you look at the writings of the most respected spiritual, psychological and scientific people today, the core of their wisdom is about listening, and then sending love. Too often we listen and care and don't utilize our access to the enormous power of God's Love.

Whether one refers to our world as having a Creator, a God, Source, Infinite Being, or Energy, there is awareness that there is a loving force. However, as we grow in consciousness, we are evolving spiritually and psychologically. Recently, there have been advances in knowledge of energy medicine, as well as the importance of what a positive belief has in our healing.

Our friend here in Prescott, Nancy Turcich, who wrote of her healing in, *Finding My Way*, has an inspiring story of healing when she crushed her spine. She lives a full life of travel, giving healing massages and sharing wisdom in her blog.

This book is about reducing much of this wisdom to stories of the basics. Years ago I was asked to write about the qualities of helping relationships. Today, I would add that a counselor, therapist, friend, workshop leader, or one who channels non-physical spirits, all listen deeply and facilitate growth within the other by what they do with what they hear. Their power is proportional to their understanding of Love and being in alignment with Love's qualities.

My goal is to enable others to trust their own special internal guidance in joyously expanding who they are. It is important to accept that we do have control over our lives. We all have choices. It is important to focus on what we want. When negative thoughts and doubts enter our minds, it is important to let them go, to transform them and then focus on a positive alternative. Hoping for another to change is wasted energy, just as beating yourself up or blaming others is fruitless. Why relive a hurt from the past when we can choose not to dwell on it, rather choose to use a good quality within to alter our old perspectives. This is where forgiveness, self compassion and being open to Spirit come in. It takes focus and work on our part to change. When you are clear about what you want, you will soon experience and accomplish more and more of that.

The followers of Abraham say it is a three-step process.

1. Ask for what you want (or pray).
2. Know that 'God' always says yes.
3. Bring yourself into alignment with whom or what you know as God.

The third step is the hardest. Notice that it doesn't say, the nicest people get what they want in life. It does say that one has to be in the flow of Spirit, to be congruent with the highest form of Love.

Jesus asked those who he healed a simple question. "Do you want to be healed?" Those who deeply did and believed were healed.

I attended a workshop given by Dr. Brugh Joy years ago where he asked me and others to 'open our hearts as we have never opened them before.'

It was life changing for me. When he and others who were deeply conscious were in alignment, the energy of their intention sent me soaring. I felt one with all, loved by Spirit and a whole and valued person.

Others, like Richard Gerber, Carolyn Myss, Ron Roth, Eckhart Tolle, Wayne Dyer, Esther Hicks (Abraham), Adyashanti, and Richard Moss, have all focused on heartfelt feelings as inner guides.

Effective counselors listen to the strongest feeling words in a session and explore them to facilitate understanding of a client's patterns that might need different choices for happier living. Staying in their pain results in clients becoming mired in it, and causing the helper to get out of positive alignment. Enabling the other to focus instead on where they want to be enables the helpee to remain balanced and connected to their own inner being. Then they can better facilitate their own choices.

A helper is not there to 'fix' another. Rather to be a person with alignment who respects the worth of who the other was created to be. Enabling the other, because of a deep love of them as one of God's creations, allows them to see the best parts of themselves.

A few years ago our cocker spaniel became ill and couldn't keep anything in her stomach. The vet gave us pills, and instructed us to get thirty ounces of fluid in her daily. Our dog clenched her teeth more tightly each day and when her mouth was forced open with a turkey baster-full of liquid, shook her head in anguish, spit some of it up and, in general, looked miserable.

We could not stand to be this abusive and my husband got down on the floor and had a heart-to-heart talk with her. He told her if it was her time to go, we would send her off with love and gratitude for our time together. If she chose life, she'd have to decide to drink and eat from her bowls.

We waited anxiously, sending lots of love energy visually as well as putting our energetic hands on her stomach. A day later she started to drink and sniff at the chicken aroma in the kitchen. She had made her decision. What a basic lesson in allowing another to make choices and not to think that to evoke change WE had to do it.

We do not change others. Our work is to turn our heads off, to meditate (a way to listen to non-physical or what we know as God). As we live a life which is an example others see and admire, we attract them to us and have the opportunity to be an example of Love.

Do you use those qualities of an evolved human to transform any negativity to positivity in your life? Qualities such as compassion, joy, kindness, forgiveness... are just a few of the ones I wear.

We all have choices to transform behaviors and attitudes. It's only a matter of changing our perspectives.

You were born with wings!

An enchanted world is one that speaks to the soul, to the mysterious depths of the heart and imagination where we find value, love, and union with the world around us. As mystics of many religions have taught, that sense of rapturous union can give a sensation of fulfillment that makes life purposeful and vibrant....

Thomas Moore

Expanding Consciousness to Better Serve Spirit

I now believe this book was waiting to be completed until I attended a workshop with Susanne Giesemann. This former Navy Commander, an aide to the Chairman of the Joint Chiefs of Staff, is now a practicing psychic-medium, and was in the Prescott area this week.

Photo from www.suzannegiesemann.com/.

Those of us who attended believe in a spiritual world where there is no end to our existence and that we all just shed our physical bodies when our earthly lives end and return to the more expansive non-physical beings we were created to be. However, did we believe that those who had passed were around us much of the time and that we could contact them? Even give and receive messages?

I wasn't sure about me, but I left the workshop with a firm belief that I, with the aid of my guides, could contact non-physicals and both give and receive messages. Wow! Talk about getting a bigger pan!

After the tragic death of her step-daughter by a bolt of lightening, Suzanne's entire life changed and she began her journey that led to now teaching and practicing mediumship.

While I previously thought that we who are still alive on this earth may harbor unsaid words, I had not realized the service mediums do for those who have passed and wish to give messages to family members and friends still alive. What pain and hurt could and does get relieved, and the path for forgiveness is created.

Many of us gulped as she challenged us to use the new tools we had just acquired. How excited I was to discover that I could do this! I was able to share with a young woman that her daughter, who had recently passed, wanted her mother to go to the beach and enjoy the water as they used to do. I received the understanding that my mother, who had been a writer in her later life, wanted me to know that she was helping me write this book. I had wished that this was so and now know it is.

More importantly, my eyes were opened and my world vision expanded to add to my understanding of who I am, and will continue to be. I am more than ever a believer that I am both human with an ego and Spirit with a soul. How even stronger to KNOW that I am the presence of Love and am in this world to give and receive Love.

And you are, too! What is your challenge to be the light of Love in your world?

The quieter you become, the more you can hear.

Ram Dass
American spiritual teacher and author

Wrapping Up...

What would life be like if what we always wanted was to give and receive love and to live with passion and experience joy?

I have come to believe that out of our ordinary lives, we can choose to see good things as miracles and become light in our world. Others will be attracted to our presence and keep an open heart. Peace can only grow from one's own heart and expand to others.

I have come to understand that my eyes are built-in cameras. I choose to see beauty, love and things that bring me joy. Negativity can pass right through. I do not have to click the shutter and keep that energy inside.

Doesn't the Bible say that Heaven is within? The miracle is the understanding, then accepting that as truth and living it. If negativity doesn't pass through, it stays inside and causes a blockage. Then it becomes harder and harder to feel love and joy until we release those old blocks.

There are many ways to do this work, but it does require understanding the power of energy, and setting an intention to do so. Dr. Bradley Nelson's books, *The Emotion Code* and *The Body Code* are insightful into recognizing and releasing blocks. The Abraham DVDs contain great wisdom for turning our lives around. Whenever we attend a prayer service, a healing service, get a massage, participate in a drumming circle, exercise, walk, or do something that fills us with joy, it pushes the negativity out.

There are many ways to release energy blockages in our minds and hearts. Throughout this book I've given you references and resources that were helpful to me. Blessings and joy as you follow your own journey and recognize the miracles in your own life.

I'll see you along the way.

- The End -

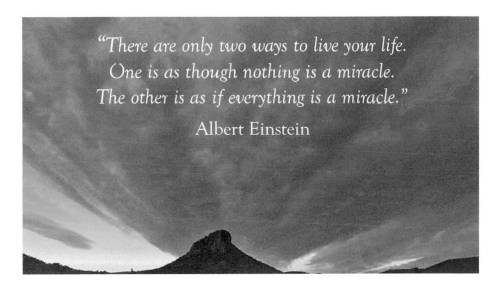

"There are only two ways to live your life.
One is as though nothing is a miracle.
The other is as if everything is a miracle."
Albert Einstein

Bibliography

A Course in Miracles, Miracles In Action Press, LLC; 1 edition, 2008.

Anthony, Lawrence. *The Elephant Whisperer: My Life with the Herd in the African Wild*, Sidgwick & Jackson Ltd, 2009.

Brown, Dan. *Da Vinci Code*, Anchor Publishing, 2009.

Bruyere, Rosalyn L. *Wheels of Light: Chakras, Auras, and the Healing Energy of the Body*, Touchstone, 1994; www.rosalynlbruyere.org/index.html; Founder, Director, and Teacher of the Healing Light Center Church.

Child, Julia, Beck, Simone, and Bertholle, Louisette. *Mastering the Art of French Cooking*, Knopf Doubleday Publishing Group, 2009.

Cohen, Andrew. *Evolutionary Enlightenment: A New Path to Spiritual Awakening*, SelectBooks; 1 edition, 2011.

Cohen, Andrew. Internet interview with Ken Wilber and Jean Houston with DC Integral Emergence, Meetup.com, www.meetup.com/kenwilber-98/messages/23881282/.

College of the Atlantic in Bar Harbor, Maine, www.coa.edu.

Federman, John. Tedxtalks.ted.com/video/TEDxHarlem-Mayor-John-Fetterman (in story, *Transformation of a Disaster*, Page 65).

Giesemann, Susanne. "A Hands-On/How-To Course in Evidence-Based Mediumship", www.suzannegiesemann.com/.

Hanh, Thich Nhat. *No Mud, No Lotus: The Art of Transforming Suffering*, Parallax Press, 2014.

Hawkins, David. *The Eye of the I*, Veritas Publishing, 2001.

Hawkins, David. *Transcending the Levels of Consciousness*, Veritas Publishing, 2007.

Hawkins, David. *Power vs Force*, Hay House, 2012.

HeartMath Institute, www.heartmath.org/.

Hempton, Gordon. SuperSoul Sunday, OprahWinfrey Network, www.supersoul.tv/supersoul-sunday/super-soul-original-short-one-mans-mission-to-record-the-earths-rarest-sounds.

Hicks, Ester. *The Law of Attraction: The Basics of the Teachings of Abraham*, Hay House, 2006.

Hicks, Esther. *The Teachings of Abraham*, Hay House, 2008.

Hicks, Esther. Abraham-Hicks Publications, www.abrahamhickslawof attraction.com/lawofattractionstore/index.html.

Hubbard, Barbara Marx. Barbaramarxhubbard.com/conscious evolution-the-next-stage-of-human-development/.

Joy, Brugh. *Joy's Way, A Map for the Transformational Journey: An Introduction to the Potentials for Healing with Body Energies*, J. P. Tarcher, Inc.; 1979.

Kaites, Elizabeth. *A Common Thread: Stories of Our Oneness*, iUniverse, 2009.

Marx Hubbard, Barbara. *Agents of Consciousness Evolution*, The Shift Network, 2012.

Maslow, Abraham. "A Theory of Human Motivation," Psychological Review, Vol 50, No 4, July 1943.

Mayle, Peter. *A Year in Provence*, Knopf Doubleday Publishing Group, 1991.

Mayes, Frances. *Under The Tuscan Sun: At Home In Italy*, Broadway Books (first published 1996).

Monk Kidd, Sue. *The Secret Life of Bees*, Viking, 2002.

Myss, Caroline. *Sacred Contracts, Awakening Your Divine Potential*, Random House Australia, 2002.

Nelson, Bradley, *The Emotion Code: How to Release Your Trapped Emotions for Abundant Health, Love and Happiness, Wellness*, Unmasked Publishing, 2007.

Nelson, Bradley. *The Body Code: A Personal Wellness and Weight Loss Plan at the World Famous Green Valley Spa*, Atria Books, New York, 2001.

People to People, Humana, www.humana.org/. Network of 32 organizations engaged in international solidarity, cooperation and development in Europe, Africa, Asia and the Americas.

Photographs of newborns, "Now I Lay Me Down to Sleep," nilmdts, Centennial, CO, www.nowilaymedowntosleep.org.

Renard, Gary R. *The Disappearance of the Universe*, Hay House, Inc., 2004.

Rohr, Richard. *Falling Upward: A Spirituality for the Two Halves of Life*, Jossey-Bass, 2011.

Rosemergy, Jim. "Making the Sun Stand Still", *The Power of Presence*, Unityonline, 2009, Page 15, http://av.unityonline.org/en/publications/pdf/thepowerofpresence.pdf).

Selby, Margaret. *Heart to Hand, An Enlightenment for the Mind, Body and Soul*, Balboa Press, Bloomington, IN, 2016.

Smith, Robin. *Hungry, The Truth About Being Full,* Hay House, 2013.

Taylor Good, Karen. *Get a Bigger Pan, on* CD *Song Guru,* Insight Records, 2004.

Taylor, Jill Bolte. Www.ted.com/talksjill_bolte_taylor_s_powerful_ stroke_of_insight?language=en.

Ted Talks (TED, Technology, Entertainment, Design, a global set of conferences run by the private nonprofit organization Sapling Foundation, under the slogan "Ideas Worth Spreading".

Tolle, Eckhart. *The Power of Now,* Namaste Publishing, 2004.

Turcich, Nancy M. *Finding My Way, From Paralysis to a Rich, Full Life,* Bez Publications, 2009.

Walsh, Neale Donald. *Conversations with God* (Book 1, G.P. Putnam's Sons, 1996.

Walsh, Neale Donald. Workshops on *Living From Your Soul,* Evolving Wisdom, 2015.

Williamson, Marianne. *A Return to Love, Reflections on the Principles of a Course in Miracles,* HarperOne, 1996.

Winfrey, Oprah. "No experience is wasted... Everything in life is happening to grow you up, to fill you up, to help you become more of who you were created to be", www.oprah.com/quote/oprah-quote-on-experience.

Winfrey, Oprah. Interview with Gordon Hempton, SuperSoul Sunday, OprahWinfrey Network, www.supersoul.tv/supersoul-sunday/super-soul-original-short-one-mans-mission-to-record-the-earths-rarest-sounds.

Winfrey, Oprah. Interview with Phil Jackson, SuperSoul Sunday, Oprah Winfrey Network, www.supersoul.tv/supersoul-sunday/soul-to-soul-with-legendary-nba-coach-phil-jackson.

Winfrey, Oprah. Interview with Sue Monk Kidd, SuperSoul Sunday, Oprah Winfrey Network, www.oprah.com/own-super-soul-sunday/Oprah-and-Book-Club-Author-Sue-Monk-Kidd-The-Soul-of-a-Writer.

Winfrey, Oprah. Interview with Dr. Robin Smith, SuperSoul TV, www.supersoul.tv/supersoul-sunday/what-dr-robin-smith-was-really-hungry-for.

Wolf, Amber (compiler). *Dr. Sid Wolf's Spiritual Healing Legacy,* Audio CD, Vision Way Publications, 2013; www.amberwolfphd.com/.

Wolf, Sidney and Wolf, Carol Melvin. *The Counseling Skills Evaluation Manual*, The Psychological Skills Development Corporation, Poway, CA. 1976.

Wolf, Sidney, Wolf, Carol Melvin and Spielberg, Gil. The *Wolf Counseling Skills Evaluation Handbook*, National Publication, 1980.

Wordsworth, William. *The Prelude*, Book 12, 208-218, 1850 edition.

Page 90
Sky Spirit Studios
354 Chief Joseph Crescent
N. Vancouver, BC V7M 1J1
www.skyspiritstudio.com
Telephone: 604-987-5590
Fax: 604-987-8576

Order Form

Placing an order for yourself or a friend is easy. Simply fill out this form and mail it with a check or money order to:

Elizabeth Kaites
Light & Love Publishing
P.O. Box 12551
Prescott, Arizona 86304

Name _____

Address _____

City _____ State _____ Zip _____

Phone _____ Cell phone _____

Email _____

Miracle Moments of Transformation

$25.00 x _____ = _____
No. of Books

A Common Thread

$17.95 x _____ = _____
No. of Books

Subtotal _____

AZ Tax (currently 5.6%) _____

Shipping/handling ($3.00 per book) _____

Total _____

Prices subject to change without notice. Please make check or money orders payable to Elizabeth Kaites. Please allow 4 to 6 weeks for delivery.

Made in the USA
Charleston, SC
23 September 2016